KT-177-861

C334515042

CLIVE GIFFORD

www.waylandbooks.co.uk

First published in Great Britain in 2020 by Wayland

Editor: Julia Adams
Designer: Rocket Design (East Anglia) Ltd
Picture researcher: Diana Morris
Artwork: pp60-61 by Bess Callard

HB ISBN 978 1 5263 1071 2
PB ISBN 978 1 5263 1072 9

Printed in Dubai

MIX
Paper from
responsible sources
FSC® C104740

Wayland
An imprint of
Hachette Children's Group
Carmelite House
50 Victoria Embankment
London EC4Y 0DZ

An Hachette UK Company
www.hachette.co.uk

Picture credits: © Airbus: 44tl.

Alamy: NG Images 59b; Pictorial Press 9tr;

Bisbos.com: 11c, 63.

Chinese Academy of Sciences/China National Space Administration/The Science and Application Center for Moon and Deepspace Exploration: 5bl.

ESA: ATG medialab 29tr, 56l; CNES/Arianespace 4c;ESA 37bl, 37tr; Starsem 6.

Lockheed Martin: 58cl.

NASA: Ames Research Center/JPL-Caltech 46cl, 46-47c; James Blair 40c; ESA 21tr, 31cr, ESA/J. Hester, A. Loll (ASU) 31br; ESA/STScl 31tr; Goddard/Chris Gunn 57bl;

John Hopkins University APL/Steve Gribben 53l; John Hopkins University APL/SW Research Institute48c, 48bl; Bill Ingalls 20l, 52l; IPAC-Caltech 51bl;JPL 25tr, 29cr, 36-37c, 38bl, 52br; JPL-Caltech 2br, 3bc, 4b, 38-39c, 39br, 47br, 49t, 51tr, 54bl,54-55, 55t, 56bc; JPL-Caltech/Ball Aerospace 47tr; JSC 15br; JPL-Caltech/CXC/SAO 51tl;JPL/Caltech/Space Science Institute 37cr; JPL-Caltech/SwRI/MSSS/Bjorn Jonsson 53r; JPL-CalTech/ UCLA/MPS/DLR/IDA 49b; Joel Kowsky 44b; Marshall Space Flight Centre 50; Commander James McDivitt: 13b; D Meltzer 12c; NASA: 2bl,5tl,5cr,7c, 9br,12bl,13t 13c,14tl,16bl,17br, 21br, 23t,23cr, 23bl, 24, 25bl,26bl, 26-27c, 27br, 29bl,30b,34l, 34-35c, 39tr,40tl,41t, 41c,41b,42cl,42-43p,44tr, 45t,45c,45b,57t,59t;NSSDC.GSFC 18-19;Tim Terry 7t; Jeff Williams 20-21.

NOAA: 28cl.

Science Photo Library: Carlos Clarivan: 14-15c.

Shutterstock: antonsav 3tr, 8-9; Zvonimir Atletic 22-23c, 62; Riko Best 7br; cxstock with elements by NASA 28-29; Everett Historical 35br; Anatoly Fedotov 11br; Ilya Genkin32-33; Robert Hardholt 15tr; IrinaK 33b; Molotok289 18bl; Nerthuz 16-17, 30-31c; Mikhail Olykainen 3cr, 10l; Vadim Orlov 8l; Photo Spirit 33t; Vadim Sadovski front cover b; Supphachai Salaeman 2-3bg; fluke samed 7bl bg; martin stuard 1; Lukasz Pawel Szczepanski 29tl;3dsculptor front cover bg; u3d 58-59.

SKA Project Development Office and Swinburne Atronomy Productions/CC Wikimedia Commons: 57br.

USAF/Los Angeles AFB: 28tl.

US National Archives: 35tr.

CONTENTS

Out of this World 4
Rocket Science 6
The First Space Satellite 8
Vostok 10
Mercury-Gemini Missions 12
Saturn V 14
Apollo Spacecraft 16
Lunar Rovers 18
Soyuz Spacecraft 20
Skylab 22
Voyager 1 and 2 24
Space Suits 26
Satellites 28
The Hubble Space Telescope 30
Radio Telescopes 32
Space Shuttle 34
Piggyback Probes 36
Mars Rovers 38
Astronaut Training 40
International Space Station 42
The ISS at Work 44
Planet Hunter: Kepler Space Telescope 46
Dwarf Planet Explorers 48
Super Scopes 50
Jupiter and Solar Probes 52
Mars 2020 54
Soon in Space 56
Space Bases 58
Build a Rocket 60
Glossary 62
Further Reading 63
Index 64

OUT OF THIS WORLD

Amazing technology has enabled people and machines to leave Earth and explore the Universe. Telescopes launched into space have given us clearer views of distant stars and galaxies while space stations provide long-term homes in space for astronauts.

LIFT OFF!

Machines and spacecraft are sent into space using powerful launch vehicles propelled by rocket engines. This Ariane 5 launch vehicle (right) is built and run by the European Space Agency (ESA) – a group of 22 European nations. In 2018, the 100th successful Ariane mission launched.

IN ORBIT

Satellites orbit the Earth and monitor the planet, as well as providing people with TV images and global navigation systems. In 2017, India launched a staggering 104 small satellites, all at the same time.

PROBING PLANETS

Astonishing space probes have flown by or landed on other planets, as well as comets and asteroids. NASA's InSight probe reached Mars in 2018 after a 6.5-month journey across 484 million kilometres of space.

InSight's twin solar panels have a total area equal to a table tennis table.

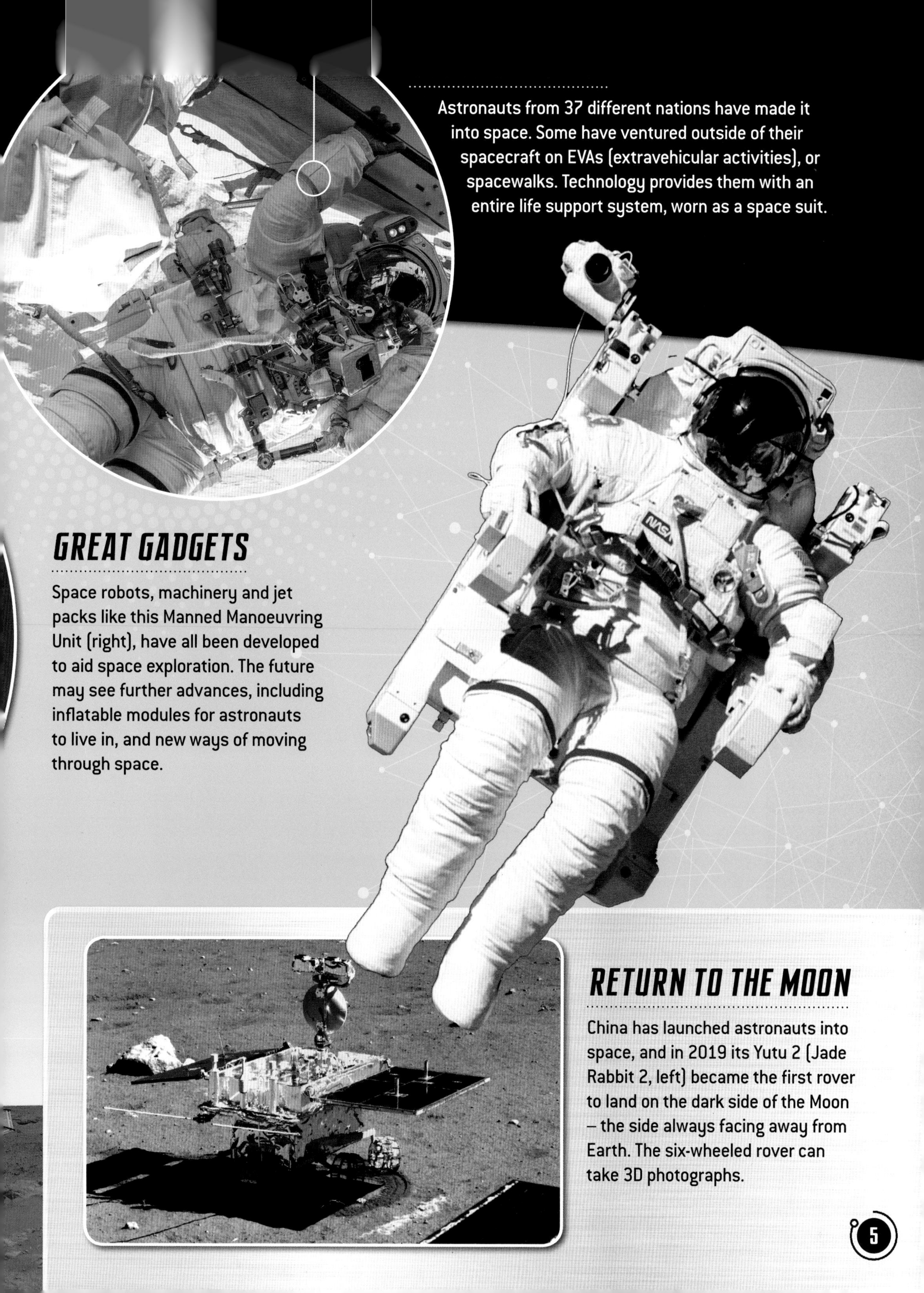

Astronauts from 37 different nations have made it into space. Some have ventured outside of their spacecraft on EVAs (extravehicular activities), or spacewalks. Technology provides them with an entire life support system, worn as a space suit.

GREAT GADGETS

Space robots, machinery and jet packs like this Manned Manoeuvring Unit (right), have all been developed to aid space exploration. The future may see further advances, including inflatable modules for astronauts to live in, and new ways of moving through space.

RETURN TO THE MOON

China has launched astronauts into space, and in 2019 its Yutu 2 (Jade Rabbit 2, left) became the first rover to land on the dark side of the Moon – the side always facing away from Earth. The six-wheeled rover can take 3D photographs.

ROCKET SCIENCE

To leave Earth and the pull of its gravity takes serious power, especially when a heavy spacecraft can weigh thousands of kilograms. Rocket engines fitted to launch vehicles generate the thrust needed to send technology into space.

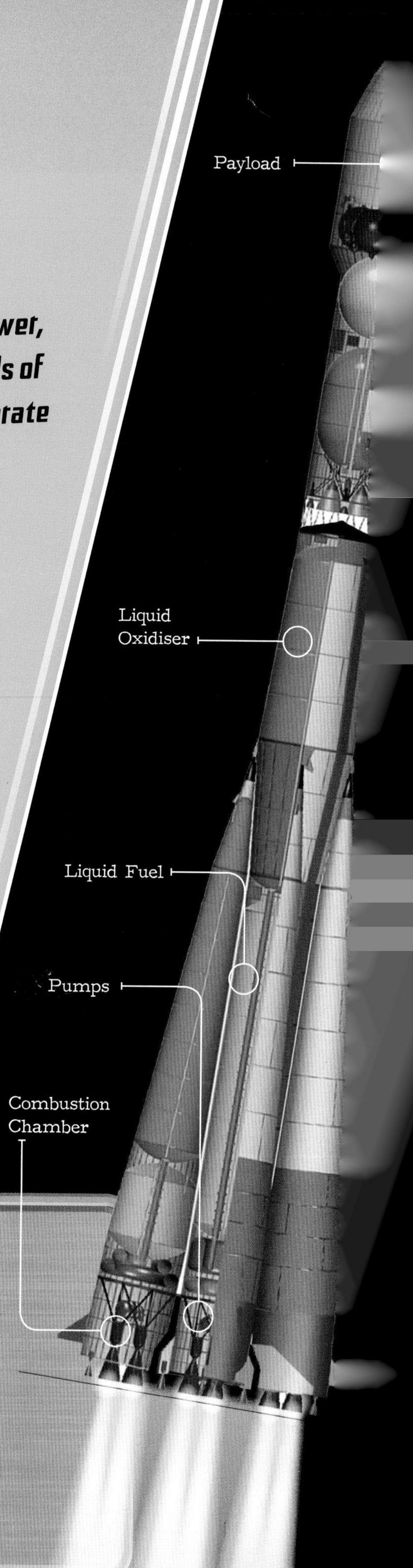

WHAT IS A ROCKET?

Many types of engines, such as petrol engines in cars and jet engines in aircraft, need oxygen from air to work. There's no air in space, but rockets get around this problem by carrying their own supply of oxygen, or an oxygen-creating substance called an oxidiser, along with their fuel.

COMBUSTION CHAMBER

The fuel and air are mixed together in the combustion chamber and burned to produce large amounts of inflating gases. These gases expand out of the nozzles at the bottom of the rocket as thrust.

ACTION AND REACTION

Rockets work according to a law of physics developed by Sir Isaac Newton. It states that for each action, there is an equal and opposite reaction. A rocket generates thrust which pushes downwards, hard against the launch pad on the ground. The launch pad pushes back with an equal force but in the opposite direction, which propels the rocket off the ground and into space.

POWER AND PAYLOAD

rge launch vehicles often contain a
ber of rocket engines which, together,
nerate enormous power. This Delta IV
avy rocket (right) can carry a payload
spacecraft, supplies or a satellite) into
ace weighing more than 20,000 kg and
generates over 955 tonnes of
thrust at lift-off.

A Delta IV Heavy rocket lifts off from Space Launch Complex 37 at Cape Canaveral Air Force Station in Florida, USA. It is carrying NASA's Orion spacecraft on an unpiloted test into Earth's orbit.

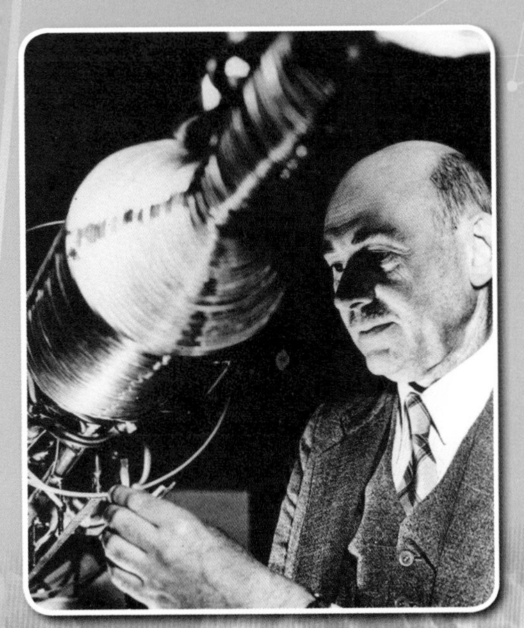

EARLY ROCKETS

Gunpowder acted as solid fuel for the first rockets, thought to have been invented in ancient China. They were used as fireworks, signalling devices and sometimes as weapons. It wasn't until the 1920s that the first rocket using liquid fuel, built by U.S. engineer Robert Goddard (left), took to the air.

WARTIME WEAPON

Early rocket flights were measured in metres, but the German V2 missile (right), first launched in 1942, had a range of 320 km and could travel over 100 km above Earth. It was used as a weapon during the Second World War (1939-45). After the war, a number of nations developed their own long-range rocket-powered missiles. Some could travel thousands of kilometres and were modified to send the first technology into space.

THE FIRST SPACE SATELLITE

SECOND STAGE

FIRST STAGE

With a diameter of 58.5 cm, Sputnik 1 was small and simple. Yet, it caused a sensation when launched in 1957, as it was the world's first artificial satellite. During its three months in space, Sputnik orbited Earth over 1,400 times. Its success signalled the start of the 'Space Race' between the former Soviet Union and the USA for supremacy in space exploration.

CONVERTED MISSILE

Sputnik was launched on top of a converted long-range missile called the R-7. It was a two-stage launch vehicle. Once the rocket engines in its first stage had used up all their fuel, that stage fell away to save weight and the engines in the second stage fired.

R-7 Rocket at the Samara Space Museum, Russia.

WHIP ANTENNA

Two pairs of radio antennas, one set 2.4 m long and the other 2.9 m long, broadcast signals from the radio transmitter at two different frequencies. Amateur radio fans all over the planet thrilled at tuning in to hear Sputnik's beeps as it circled the Earth.

SPUTNIK 2 AND 3

Two further Sputniks were launched successfully. Both were cone-shaped spacecraft and much larger than Sputnik 1. Sputnik 3 took a laboratory of science instruments into space, while Sputnik 2 carried a dog, called Laika, to become the first mammal to orbit the Earth. In 1958, the US successfully launched their first satellite, Explorer 1.

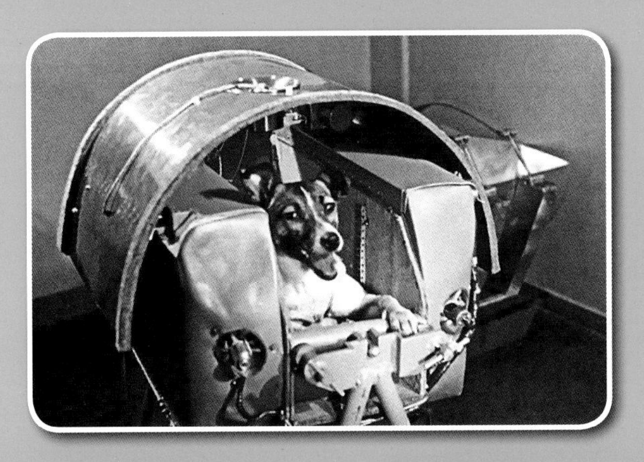

Sputnik 2 weighed 508.3 kg, 6 kg of which was its passenger, Laika, who was supplied with oxygen, food and water within the craft.

BOLTED AND SEALED

Sputnik's case was constructed in two halves which were fitted together and held in place by airtight seals and 36 bolts. The inside of the satellite was filled with nitrogen gas.

POLISHED SPHERE

The outer casing was made of 2-mm-thick aluminium. It was covered in a heat-resistant aluminium-magnesium-titanium alloy, polished so that it reflected sunlight.

The outer layer protected an inner casing and inside that, 51 kg of batteries and radio transmitters. The batteries powered the radio's signals for 21 days before running out.

Sputnik 1's construction featured an outer heat shell acting as the heat shield and an inner shell housing the batteries and transmitters.

FAN-TASTIC

Inside the satellite an electric fan was connected to a simple temperature sensor switch which turned on the fan if the interior temperature rose above 36 °C.

VOSTOK

In April 1961, Yuri Gagarin left Earth and became the first person in space. His historic mission was undertaken in a Soviet Vostok spacecraft that orbited at a height of between 187 km and 327 km above Earth. Gagarin's mission may have only lasted 108 minutes, but its impact was felt around the world.

DESCENT CAPSULE

This 2.3-m-diameter steel ball was protected by a heat shield. When the capsule re-entered Earth's atmosphere, friction caused it to heat up to temperatures of over 2,500 °C.

EJECTION SEAT

Gagarin lay strapped to an ejection seat. At an altitude above ground of around 7,000 m, the ejection seat fired him clear of the spacecraft. At around 2,500 m, a parachute opened and he floated safely back to Earth.

ROCKET LAUNCH

The Vostok spacecraft was sent into orbit by the Vostok 8K72K launch vehicle. Developed from an R-7 long-range missile, this rocket stood 38.36 m tall with its payload and weighed 281,375 kg. Six and a half minutes after lift-off, the rocket's fuel was used up and it fell away, leaving the Vostok spacecraft to head into orbit.

AIR SUPPLY

Sixteen spherical tanks fitted to the outside of the craft stored either oxygen or nitrogen. They supplied the descent capsule with air for breathing, as well as oxygen for the rocket engine housed in the instrument module.

Four booster rockets provided the Vostok 8K72K with extra power at lift-off.

LOOKING OUT

The craft had three glass portholes as windows, but no controls, as the mission was run from the ground. Gagarin could view instrument panels showing the temperature and air pressure inside Vostok using a mirror sewn into the sleeve of his space suit.

TALKING BACK

A series of radio antennas kept Gagarin in touch with mission control back on Earth. In total, the spacecraft contained more than 15,000 m of wiring.

INSTRUMENT MODULE

Vostok's instrument module housed power supplies and a rocket engine. It was joined to the descent capsule by steel bands which were broken near the end of the mission to allow the descent module to return to Earth on its own.

RETURNING HERO

From hundreds of original recruits, Yuri Gagarin was chosen after arduous training and selection tests. He became a global celebrity after his historic mission – far too important to be risked again on a spaceflight. Two years after his mission, Valentina Tereshkova, also flying in a Vostok spacecraft, became the first woman in space.

ЧЕЛОВЕК В
КАПИТАН ПЕРВОГО ЗВЕЗДО

MERCURY-GEMINI MISSIONS

Spurred on by Yuri Gagarin's successful flight, NASA launched its Mercury spacecraft less than a month later. Inside, Alan Shepard became the first US astronaut. Five further Mercury missions were flown before Gemini, capable of holding two astronauts, took over.

MERCURY

At just 2 m long and 1.89 m in diameter, the cone-shaped spacecraft contained no computers but a lot of controls for the astronaut to master. These included 55 electrical switches and 35 mechanical levers.

ENTRY HATCH

The astronaut entered Mercury through a small doorway while wearing a silver pressure space suit. Inside, there was a window and a periscope which gave a view below the astronaut's feet.

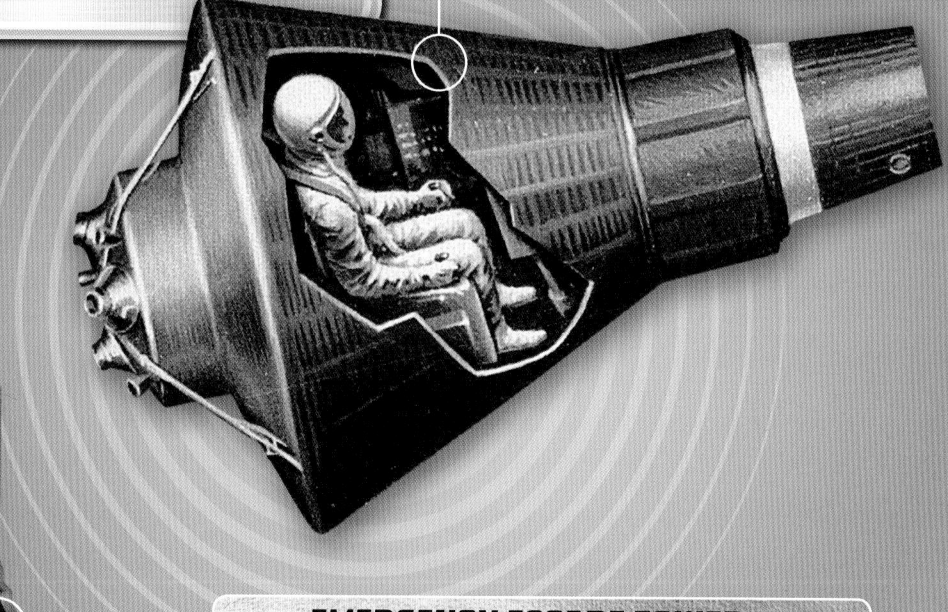

EMERGENCY ESCAPE TOWER

Fitted to Mercury's nose, this could lift the capsule away from its launch vehicle if there were problems shortly after lift-off. Once high enough, parachutes would open to return the spacecraft safely back to Earth.

Gordon Cooper piloted the last Mercury spaceflight, Mercury-Atlas 9, in 1963. During that 34-hour mission he became the first American to spend an entire day in space.

GEMINI SPACECRAFT

Ten Gemini spacecraft carried astronauts into space between 1963 and 1966. They helped pave the way for the Apollo landings on the Moon (see pages 16-17).

Four NASA astronauts pose with the Gemini spacecraft, including Edwin 'Buzz' Aldrin (bottom left) who would be one of the first two men on the Moon.

CABIN AREA

Each astronaut had their own entry-exit hatch and sat in a moulded seat for the whole mission, the longest of which, Gemini 7, lasted 13 days, 18 hours.

TWIN MODULES

Gemini was 5.6 m long and featured an equipment module at the rear and a re-entry module carrying two astronauts. The two separated before the re-entry module returned to Earth.

SPACEWALK AND RENDEZVOUS

In 1965, Ed White became the first American to undertake an EVA, spending 20 minutes in space outside his Gemini 4 craft. The same year, Gemini 6 and 7 met in space, manoeuvring to within metres of each other using radar systems fitted inside the spacecrafts' noses.

White made his spacewalk attached via a 7.6-m-long tether which also supplied him with oxygen and radio communications.

SATURN V

The heavier a spacecraft is or the further away from Earth it must travel, the more power required to launch it. The Apollo missions that carried astronauts to the Moon needed huge amounts of power at lift-off and the world's biggest launch vehicle, the Saturn V, proved just the job.

BIG BEAST

Standing 110.6 m tall (or the height of the average 35-floor building), a Saturn V at launch weighed around 2.8 million kg or the weight of more than 400 African elephants. Thirteen Saturn Vs were launched successfully between 1967 and 1973.

SECOND STAGE

After less than three minutes, the first stage's fuel was all used up and it fell away, by which time the Saturn V was some 68 km above the ground. The five J2 engines in the second stage fired to push the rocket further away from Earth.

FIRST STAGE

This stage held five F1 rocket engines as well as 770,000 litres of kerosene fuel and 1.2 million litres of liquid oxygen. The kerosene and oxygen were pumped and mixed together before being burned by the engines to get the whole, heavy, launch vehicle off the ground.

PAYLOAD

The craft carried into space, such as the Apollo spacecraft or the Skylab space station, sat at the top of the rocket, covered by protective panels, known as fairings.

F1 ROCKET ENGINE

Each F1 engine stood 5.7 m tall and delivered an incredible 691,818 kg of thrust – more than all three main engines on a space shuttle. Together, the five F1 engines consumed over 13 tonnes of fuel and oxygen every second.

THIRD STAGE

A little over nine minutes after lift-off, the third stage took over and propelled the spacecraft to its desired orbit. Measuring 17.8 m tall by 6.6 m in diameter, the third stage contained a single J2 rocket engine.

ON ITS WAY

Each Saturn V was put together in NASA's giant Vehicle Assembly Building. It was then carried, along with its launch tower, by a giant crawler transporter (right). At the time, this was the biggest land vehicle in the world but moved slowly, inching along at speeds of under 1.6 km/h.

APOLLO SPACECRAFT

In July 1969, Neil Armstrong and Edwin 'Buzz' Aldrin became the first humans to set foot on the Moon, an average of 384,400 km away from Earth. They reached their target in the Apollo 11 Lunar Module (LM), one part of a complex Apollo spacecraft.

SERVICE MODULE

This 7.49-m-long module contained a rocket engine which placed the spacecraft in orbit around the Moon, 110 km from its surface. The Service Module also supplied oxygen, water and electric power to the Command Module.

COMMAND MODULE

One astronaut remained in this module at all times. On the return journey, the Command and Service Modules separated and the Command Module carried the astronauts back to Earth.

SPLASHDOWN

The Command Module was carried back to Earth suspended below three large parachutes. The craft landed in the Pacific Ocean, staying afloat with the aid of flotation bags.

Apollo 11 crew and a Navy diver await pickup from the USS Hornet after splashdown.

LUNAR MODULE ASCENT STAGE

This cabin was the astronauts' home whilst on the Moon and just large enough to sling hammocks up to sleep in. When leaving the Moon, a rocket engine fired, powering the descent stage away and leaving the ascent stage on the Moon.

APOLLO GUIDANCE COMPUTER

Despite possessing just 1/500,000th of the memory of a modern 32 GB smartphone, this 31 kg computer was ingeniously programmed to help handle Apollo's complex manoeuvres in space.

LUNAR MODULE DESCENT STAGE

With its engine and tank holding 8,200 kg of fuel, protected from temperature extremes by gold foil, the Descent Module also featured length-adjustable legs ending in wide footpads. One leg carried the ladder that the astronauts climbed down to reach the Moon's surface.

Astronaut Edwin 'Buzz' Aldrin Jr. descends the steps of the Lunar Module (LM) ladder as he prepares to walk on the Moon.

DOCKING

When the Command and Lunar Modules were docked, astronauts crawled through a 76-cm-wide tunnel to travel between the modules. Both the Lunar and Service Modules were jettisoned before the Command Module could return to Earth.

LUNAR ROVERS

Driveable moon buggies, called Lunar Roving Vehicles (LRV), were carried by the Apollo 15, 16 and 17 missions to the Moon in 1971 and 1972. These 3.1-m-long, two-person vehicles had a top speed of 13 km/h and helped astronauts explore a lot further than they could on foot.

BACK TO EARTH

This large dish made of wire mesh folded out to act as a powerful radio antenna to send TV images from the rover's camera back to Earth.

COLOUR CAMERA

The large colour TV camera could be remote-operated by NASA mission control on Earth. It was used to film the Apollo Lunar Module blasting off the Moon on its return to Earth.

LUNOKHOD 1 AND 2

These two large unmanned rovers reached the Moon in 1970 and 1972. Their large, tub-shaped bodies ran on eight wheels. A lid on the tub hinged open to angle solar panels towards the Sun during the day to generate power. At night, the lid closed to keep the rover's electronics warm. The rovers each operated for many months and sent a total of 100,000 TV pictures of the Moon back to Earth.

BATTERY-OPERATED

The two 36-volt batteries powered the rover's electrical systems, including the four wheel-motors. Each motor generated 0.25 hp – less than 1/400th of the power of the engine in a family car.

WEBBED SEATS

Aluminium tubing seats were covered in nylon webbing and featured seat belt straps fixed by Velcro. A large container under the seats let the astronauts store Moon rocks, pebbles and dust samples.

TOOL CADDY

A carrier at the rear held hand tools including a rake, a scoop and brushes for use by the astronauts on the Moon's surface when they collected rock samples. The Apollo 15 astronauts collected 76.7 kg of Moon rocks.

DUSTGUARDS

Protective mudguards stopped dust from the Moon's surface billowing up over the astronauts and the rover's instruments. When one of these was damaged during the Apollo 17 mission, astronauts used laminated maps and strong sticky tape to make a new one.

SOYUZ SPACECRAFT

This durable spacecraft was first launched in 1967. It has outlasted many other spacecraft and gone through many modifications since. The latest version, Soyuz MS, has advanced computing, LED lighting and upgraded communications systems.

ORBITAL MODULE

This module holds the main living quarters for three astronauts and includes a toilet. It can support life in space for up to 30 days.

SOLAR CELLS

Solar panels give the Soyuz MS a width of 10.6 m and generate electricity, stored in five large batteries, for the space station's computer and other electronics.

LAUNCH

A Soyuz FG launch vehicle weighing 305,000 kg carries a Soyuz MS spacecraft into space.

DOCKING MECHANISM

This antenna is part of the Kurs-NA system that uses radio signals and computers to automatically guide the spacecraft to its docking target.

DESCENT MODULE

Astronauts strap themselves in inside this cramped module for both launches and return trips to Earth from space. A journey from the ISS to Earth can take as little as 3.5 hours.

INSTRUMENTATION MODULE

This weighs 2,900 kg at launch, including 800 kg of fuel and oxidiser for its 14 pairs of jet thrusters. These allow the Soyuz to change direction in space.

It's a snug fit for three astronauts inside the Soyuz Orbital Module before blast-off. The module has just 5 m^3 of living space.

A Soyuz docks with the International Space Station (ISS). A spare Soyuz is always left attached to the ISS as an emergency life raft.

SKYLAB

Most spacecraft carrying astronauts travel on missions lasting a week or two. Space stations orbit Earth and enable people to spend longer periods in space. Skylab was America's first space station and was launched by a Saturn V rocket in 1973. Astronauts spent 171 days in space on-board the spacecraft which orbited 434,442 km above the planet until it broke up and fell to Earth in 1979.

APOLLO TELESCOPE MOUNT

The Apollo Telescope Mount was an observatory fitted with a number of different telescopes all studying the Sun. A staggering 150,000 images were taken by the telescopes on film. The film canisters had to be retrieved by astronauts performing spacewalks outside of Skylab.

ORBITAL WORKSHOP

This module was the main living and working area of the space station. Crews of three astronauts performed over 2,000 hours of science experiments here, as well as exercising on a bike they were strapped onto, to avoid floating away in microgravity.

DOCKING PORTS

Located at the front of the space station, these allowed up to two Apollo spacecraft to dock (join up) with Skylab to enable astronauts to travel to and leave the space station.

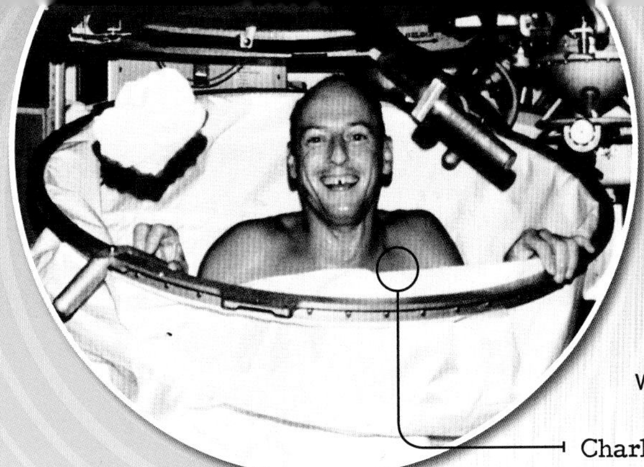

SPACE SHOWER

Skylab gave astronauts something they'd never had in space before – a shower! Showering in microgravity took over two hours, including fitting the tubular shower screen and vacuuming up floating water droplets afterwards.

Charles Conrad, Jr. enjoys a welcome hot shower in the crew quarters of the Skylab space station.

SOLAR SAILS

Power for Skylab's electrical system was provided by large solar sails filled with photovoltaic cells, which convert sunlight into electricity.

SNACKS IN SPACE

Skylab was the first spacecraft to feature a fridge and freezer, and astronauts had a choice of 72 different food items. Each astronaut filled one of these deep metal trays with pouches or tins of food, then clipped the tray to a central pillar to form a simple dining table (below).

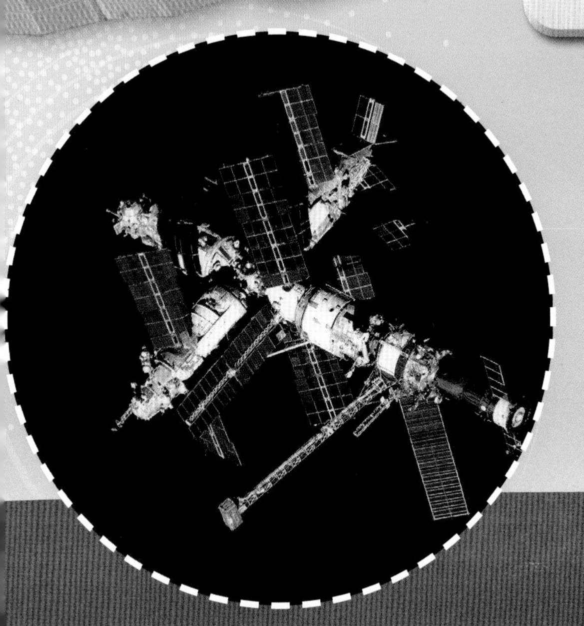

SOVIET SPACE STATIONS

The former Soviet Union (and, after its break-up, Russia) launched a number of experimental Salyut space stations in the 1970s and Mir in 1986. Mir was the largest object in space until the arrival of the ISS and like the ISS, was built up of different modules, assembled in space.

VOYAGER 1 AND 2

In 1977, two space probes were launched within 16 days of each other on a long, long journey to the outer planets in the Solar System. They're still going! By March 2019, Voyager 2 was over 17.9 billion kilometres from Earth. Voyager 1 is even more distant – 21.5 billion km away. That's more than 140 times the average distance between Earth and the Sun.

CAMERAS

Located on a boom are two TV cameras. When the probes discovered a giant storm on Neptune, thousands of kilometres wide and subsequently named the Great Dark Spot, these provided the first visual evidence.

TRIUMPH OF ENGINEERING

The Voyager probes were built before microcomputing technology was common, so used a tape recorder to store data, rather than computer memory. Despite being staggeringly complicated and made of 65,000 parts, the probes continue to work. In 2017, NASA engineers test-fired jet thrusters on Voyager 1 for the first time in 37 years – and they still worked!

WHIP ANTENNA

A pair of these 10-m-long antennas listens out for radio waves from other parts of the Universe.

EPIC TREK

The two Voyager probes explored parts of the Solar System never encountered before. They flew by and photographed Jupiter, Saturn, Uranus and Neptune, as well as 48 moons including Europa, Titan, Triton and Io.

In 1989, Voyager 2 became the first space probe to get up close and personal with Neptune, taking hundreds of photos of the Solar System's most distant planet.

HIGH-GAIN ANTENNA

This 3.7-m-diameter dish needs to be so large due to the vast distances from Earth that the probe roams. Currently, it takes more than 19 hours for a signal to be sent from Voyager 1 to reach Earth.

MAGNETOMETER BOOM

This 13-m-long structure holds scientific instruments which measure the magnetic fields that surround planets and some moons.

GOLDEN DISK

Mounted to each probe's body is a 30-cm-diameter gold disk in case the probe encounters aliens. The disk contains 115 images of Earth, 90 minutes of music and sounds from Earth including greetings in 55 different languages. Its outer case features pictures of the Sun's location in space.

SPACE SUITS

Space suits consist of many layers that are tough, fireproof and protect astronauts from the hazards of space if they venture outside of their craft. They act as a complete life support system, providing air or oxygen to breathe and protection against radiation from the Sun and the wild temperature swings in space.

EMU SUIT

NASA's Extravehicular Mobility Unit (EMU) space suit, with the occasional upgrade, has been in use by astronauts for over 35 years and is found on the ISS. It comes in an upper and lower half which join together via a bearing, sealing the astronaut inside yet still allowing them to turn at the waist.

GLOVES

Gloves interlock with the suit's wrists via a bearing. As astronauts may experience temperatures in space below -150 °C, small heaters are fitted to the glove's fingertips to help protect those body parts most vulnerable to the cold.

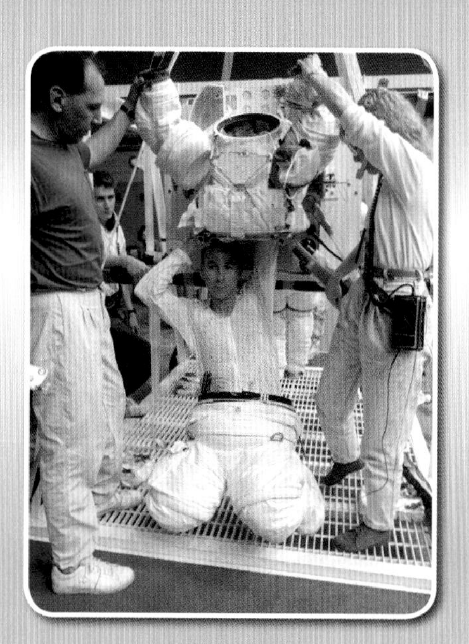

SUITING UP

It can take over an hour to suit up, starting with putting on an adult nappy (the Maximum Absorption Garment, or MAG) and liquid-cooled underwear layers which contain over 90 m of tubes. All suits are white to reflect as much heat as possible, although some come with a coloured band on their limbs to identify a particular astronaut.

SOFT SHOE SHUFFLE

Boots have soft soles to prevent damage to antennas and other delicate spacecraft parts as the astronaut moves around. The heel has a fitting to attach the astronaut to the end of a robot arm when spacewalking.

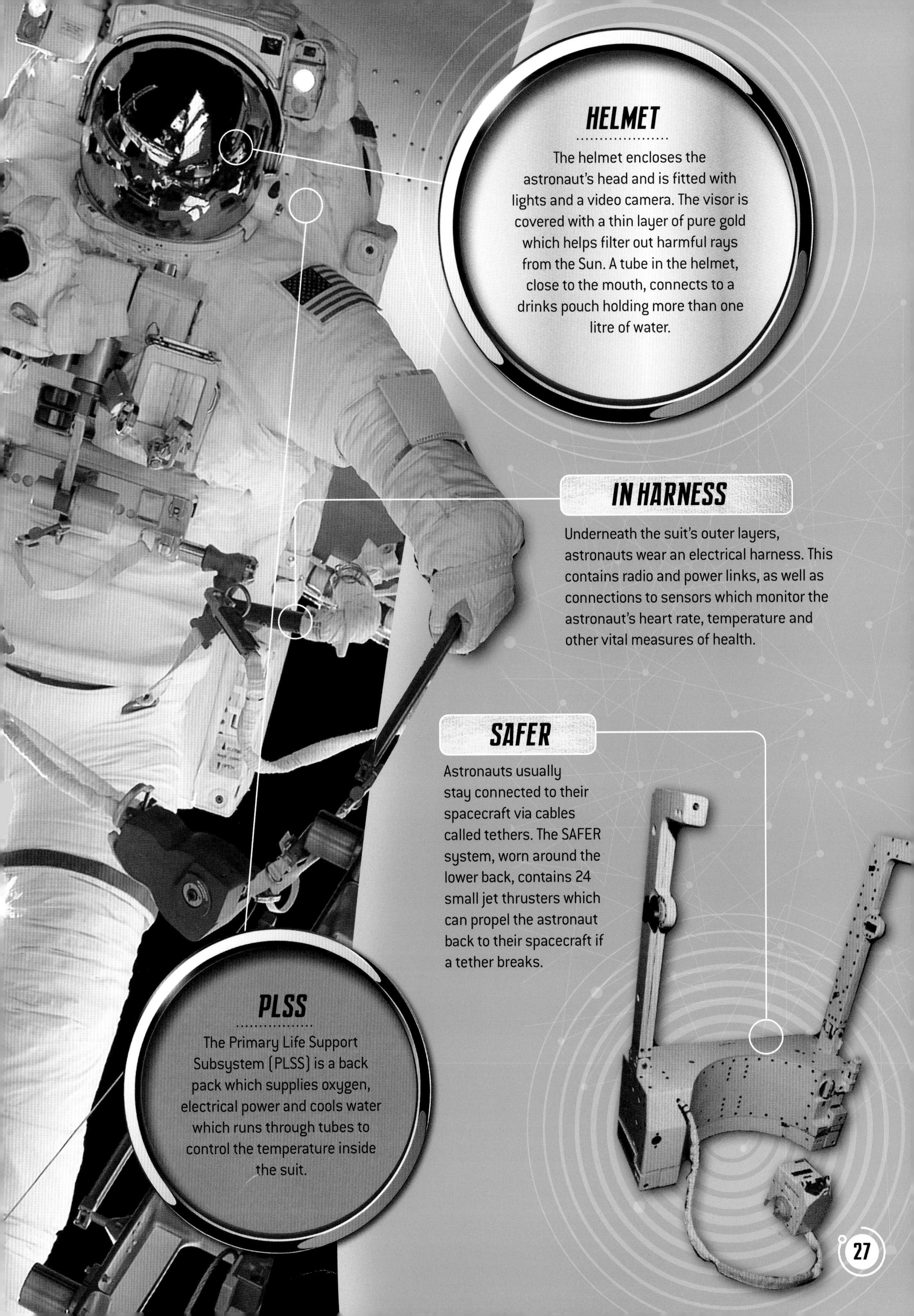

HELMET

The helmet encloses the astronaut's head and is fitted with lights and a video camera. The visor is covered with a thin layer of pure gold which helps filter out harmful rays from the Sun. A tube in the helmet, close to the mouth, connects to a drinks pouch holding more than one litre of water.

IN HARNESS

Underneath the suit's outer layers, astronauts wear an electrical harness. This contains radio and power links, as well as connections to sensors which monitor the astronaut's heart rate, temperature and other vital measures of health.

SAFER

Astronauts usually stay connected to their spacecraft via cables called tethers. The SAFER system, worn around the lower back, contains 24 small jet thrusters which can propel the astronaut back to their spacecraft if a tether breaks.

PLSS

The Primary Life Support Subsystem (PLSS) is a back pack which supplies oxygen, electrical power and cools water which runs through tubes to control the temperature inside the suit.

SATELLITES

Thousands of satellites orbit Earth performing dozens of useful roles – from making maps and forecasting the weather to photographing Earth and spying on military or industrial locations on the ground.

This communications satellite uses antennas to capture broadcast signals and then transmit them to other regions of Earth.

STAYING IN PLACE

A geostationary satellite orbits Earth around 35,780 km above the planet's equator. It moves at the same rate at which Earth is spinning, and in the same direction. As a result, it appears to hover in the same place above Earth, making it ideal to relay telephone, TV or internet signals from one part of the planet to another.

LAND, SEA AND AIR

Many satellites monitor Earth's surface, measuring land and water pollution, changing land use and even the amount of moisture in soil. Some, like the GOES-16 satellite (above), measure lightning strikes and ocean currents and temperatures. The Terra satellite, launched in 1999, can even spot forest fires in remote areas and alert fire-fighters.

SHOT DOWN

In 2008, the United States shot down its own spy satellite, USA-193! The satellite was in a decaying orbit, meaning that it was falling towards Earth, so it was destroyed by a missile above the Earth's atmosphere.

POLAR ORBITS

Satellites in polar orbit fly over the North and South Poles. These satellites fly over all of the planet's surface, strip by strip, as the Earth turns. Such orbits are used by some weather forecasting and climate monitoring satellites.

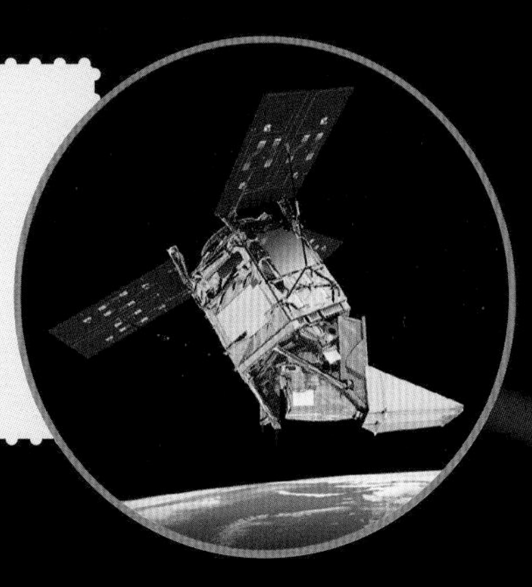

The Sentinel-5P satellite measures climate change in the Earth's atmosphere as it travels on its polar orbit.

Three space shuttle astronauts capture an Intelsat VI satellite to fit a new engine before it is returned to its orbit.

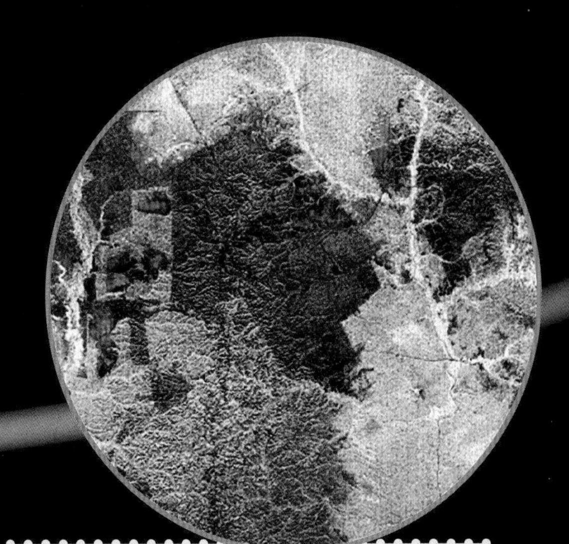

This Landsat image of Sumatra in Indonesia maps the large areas of forest (in pink and purple) that have been cleared for farming.

OUT OF HARM'S WAY

When a satellite ceases to function or is no longer needed, its controllers often instruct it to fire its thrusters, placing it in a 'graveyard orbit' – an orbit high above other working satellites.

LANDSAT

Landsat satellites operated by NASA and the U.S. Geological Service have been measuring and taking images of Earth since 1972. The latest, Landsat 8, creates images of the entire Earth once every 16 days which it downloads to computer servers for analysis.

THE HUBBLE SPACE TELESCOPE

POWER PANELS

Two 7.1 m x 2.6 m solar panels produce up to 5,500 watts of electricity which is stored in batteries. These provide power when the telescope's orbit takes it out of the line of the Sun and behind Earth.

Earth's atmosphere can distort and blur views of space for telescopes on the ground. So, some telescopes have been flown into space. The most famous of all is the Hubble Space Telescope (HST) which was launched in 1990 and is still orbiting and observing, 537,541 km above Earth.

LETTING LIGHT IN

A door opens to let the 2.4-m-diameter mirror, which weighs 828 kg, gather in light from space. The mirror reflects the light to a secondary mirror which bounces it to scientific instruments inside the telescope.

SERVICE MISSIONS

Five missions have seen astronauts repair, upgrade or add new instruments to the telescope. Here, a new spectrograph – an instrument that measures which chemicals are found in a body in space – is fitted to the Hubble. As a result of all the repairs and upgrades, the Hubble has put on weight – 1,361 kg to be precise.

DATA ANTENNA

The Hubble sends back pictures and measurements to Earth via this radio antenna. On average, the Hubble transmits 18 gigabytes of information to Earth every week.

BODY AND FRAME

The 13.2-m-long telescope's aluminium body is covered in a blanket which protects it from temperature extremes in space.

SNAPS FROM SPACE

The Hubble has been remarkably productive. It has taken more than 1.3 million observations of planets, stars and galaxies in space and has revolutionised what we know about the Universe.

'Mystic Mountain' - part of a giant gas and dust cloud called the Carina Nebula.

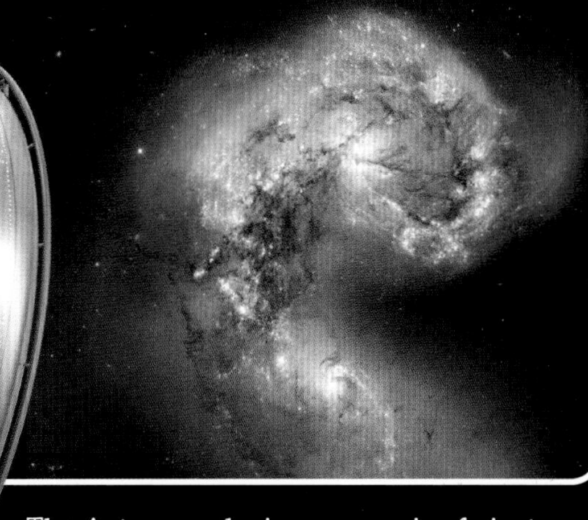

The Antenna galaxies are a pair of giant collections of stars that are merging together.

This startling image is of the remains of an exploded star called a supernova.

RADIO TELESCOPES

Many bodies in space, including planets, stars and galaxies, give off radio waves. These travel at the speed of light (around 300,000 km per second) through space and can be collected by devices called radio telescopes. Radio waves travel through dust and gas clouds in space so they can reveal stars, planets and galaxies that optical telescopes cannot see.

GATHERING WAVES

Radio waves from space are often collected in large bowls called parabolic dishes. The waves are reflected, processed and turned into a radio image that astronomers can study and learn much from. The large radio telescope at Australia's Parkes Observatory (right), has discovered more than half of all the spinning stars, called pulsars, that we know of.

Radio waves reflect off the main dish towards a device called a sub-reflector. This bounces the radio waves to central collecting spots in the main dish called feed horns.

The radio waves are then processed and a picture formed of them by a device called a receiver, before they are sent for storage and analysis on a computer.

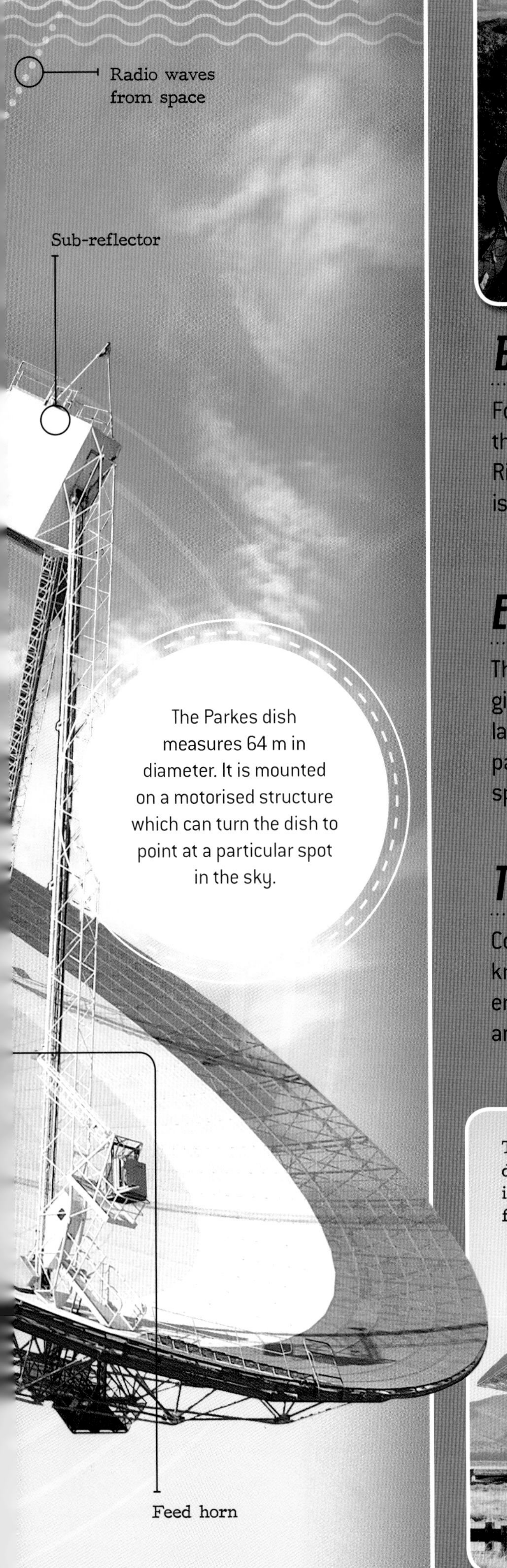

The Parkes dish measures 64 m in diameter. It is mounted on a motorised structure which can turn the dish to point at a particular spot in the sky.

BIG, BIG DISH

For over 50 years, the world's largest radio telescope was at the Arecibo Observatory on the Caribbean island of Puerto Rico (above). Its gigantic dish measured 305 m wide, which is the length of three full-sized football pitches.

EVEN BIGGER DISH

The FAST telescope in China began observations in 2016. Its gigantic 500-m-diameter dish is built into a natural basin in the landscape and is made up of over 4,000 triangular aluminium panels. Within its first months of operating it discovered two spinning stars, called pulsars.

TELESCOPE ARRAYS

Collections of radio telescopes all working together are known as arrays. By working as one big telescope, they enable astronomers to explore objects farther out into space and in more detail.

The Very Large Array in New Mexico, USA, is made up of 27 dishes, each of which is 25 m wide. The telescopes are arranged in a Y-shape and mounted on rails, allowing them to be moved further apart to work a little like a zoom lens on a camera.

SPACE SHUTTLE

NASA's small fleet of reusable spacecraft flew 133 successful missions between 1981 and 2011. In total, the 37.2-m-long shuttles flew 826.7 million km, carrying 355 different astronauts into space, as well as thousands of kilograms of space station parts, probes, satellites and space telescopes.

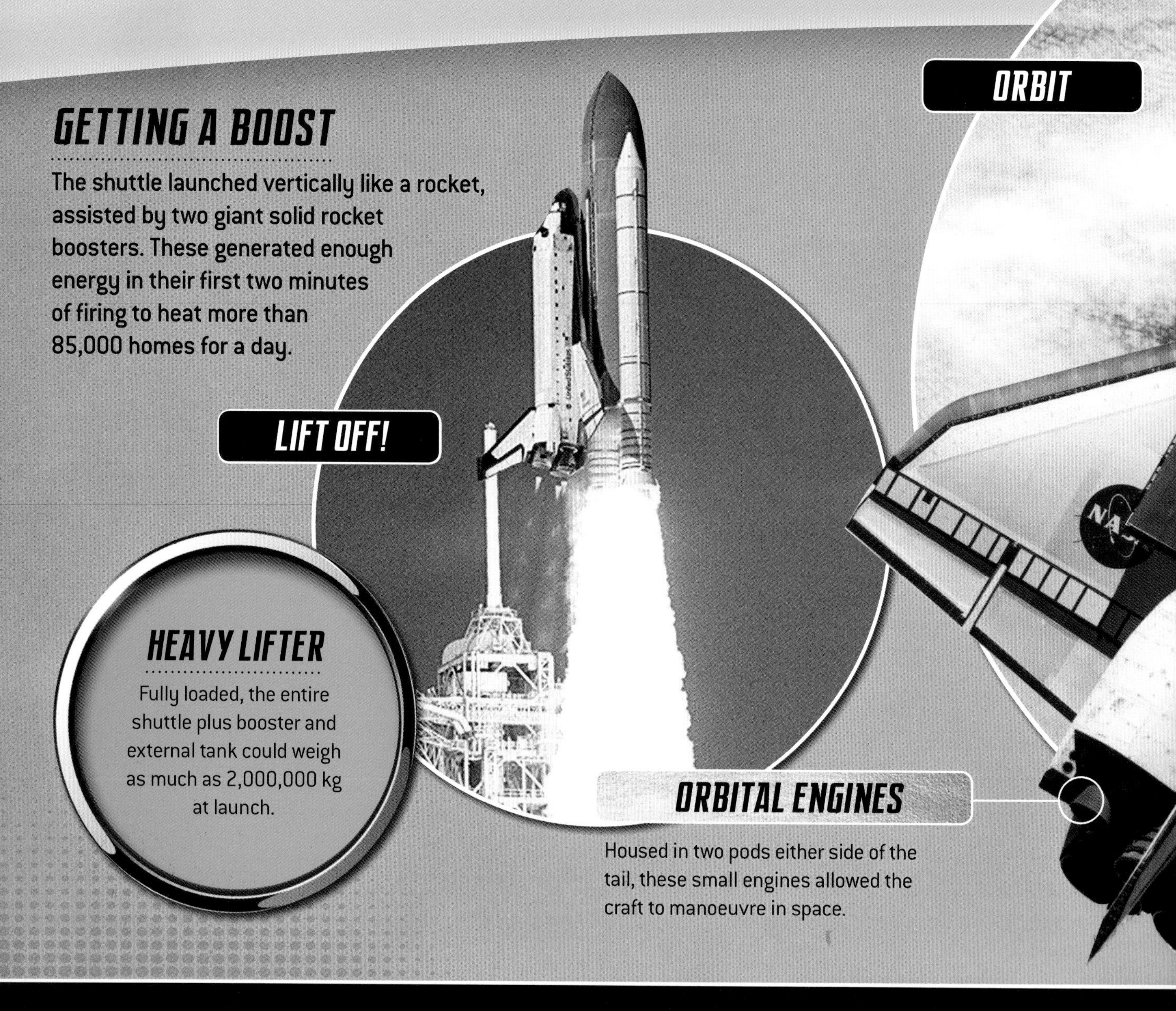

GETTING A BOOST

The shuttle launched vertically like a rocket, assisted by two giant solid rocket boosters. These generated enough energy in their first two minutes of firing to heat more than 85,000 homes for a day.

HEAVY LIFTER

Fully loaded, the entire shuttle plus booster and external tank could weigh as much as 2,000,000 kg at launch.

ORBITAL ENGINES

Housed in two pods either side of the tail, these small engines allowed the craft to manoeuvre in space.

THE SUPER SIX

Six shuttles were built between 1976 and 1992. Enterprise was a test machine but the other five all flew missions into space.

ENTERPRISE
1976

COLUMBIA
1981

THERMAL TILES

More than 25,000 silica tiles covered the craft's outer surface, protecting it from high temperatures experienced during re-entry into the Earth's atmosphere.

PAYLOAD BAY

This 18 m by 4.6 m cargo area was big enough to hold the Hubble Space Telescope and entire modules of the International Space Station.

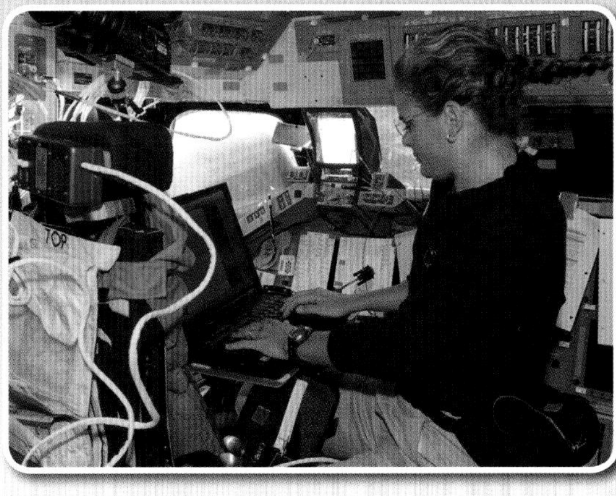

Canadian Space Agency astronaut Julie Payette uses a computer on the flight deck of space shuttle Endeavour.

FLIGHT DECK

The shuttle was controlled from the flight deck with seats and living space for the crew below. A typical crew consisted of five astronauts, although some missions carried up to eight.

LANDING

After re-entering the Earth's atmosphere, the shuttle used its rudder and hinged flaps at the back of each wing to steer as it descended and landed like an aircraft. A drag chute helped slow the craft down on the runway.

TOUCH DOWN

CHALLENGER
1983

DISCOVERY
1984

ATLANTIS
1985

ENDEAVOUR
1992

PIGGYBACK PROBES

Some missions fly a space probe to orbit a body in space, but carry a second probe which they release to land on a planet, moon or comet. These piggyback probes have allowed close-up exploration of space.

CASSINI-HUYGENS

This major mission spent 13 years orbiting Saturn, studying the planet and discovering six new moons. In 2004, Cassini released a separate space probe called Huygens. It spent three weeks travelling to Saturn's moon Titan before it parachuted down on to its surface.

SCIENTIFIC INSTRUMENTS

Cassini carried over a dozen scientific instruments which collected measurements and data about Saturn and its moons. They included an 11-m-long boom which measured Saturn's magnetic field.

HIGH GAIN ANTENNA

This large dish beamed back data gathered by Cassini's scientific instruments. Information sent from Cassini as radio signals took about 67 minutes to reach Earth.

HUYGENS PROBE

Carried to Saturn on Cassini's side, Huygens measured the gases in Titan's atmosphere as it descended. The 1.3-m-diameter probe took images of Titan's surface and continued to take measurements for 90 minutes after it landed.

PROBE POWER

Cassini featured one main engine and an identical spare main engine as back-up. In addition, 16 small jet thrusters could be fired to steer the probe when it changed course through space.

In total, Cassini took 453,048 images of Saturn, its rings and its moons.

ROSETTA-PHILAE

Built by the European Space Agency, this pair of probes took 10 years to travel 6.4 billion km to reach a comet called 67P/C-G. While Rosetta orbited the comet's nucleus, Philae (left) landed on its surface to examine what the comet was made of.

MARS ROVERS

Rovers are mobile robots that move around the surface of a planet or moon to explore and study it. A handful of rovers have been sent hundreds of millions of kilometres away to reach and travel around the planet Mars, the first being Sojourner in 1997.

SOJOURNER

Sojourner travelled to Mars inside the Pathfinder space probe which opened its panels out like a flower's petals to release the 63-cm-long rover. A small solar panel on the rover's roof generated around 15 watts of power. The rover lasted 85 days as it travelled 100 m on Mars.

MULTI CAMERAS

The rover features 17 different cameras (Sojourner had just three), used for exploration, navigation and close-up photography. All images are beamed back to Earth using a radio antenna.

MARS CURIOSITY ROVER

This car-sized rover weighs 899 kg and reached Mars in 2012. It features a weather station and an entire lab's worth of scientific tools and instruments to study the surface of the planet. These include Chemcam which fires a laser to turn rock into gas. Curiosity then analyses the gas to see whether it contains chemicals vital for life to exist.

EXPLORING ARM

A 2.1-m-long robot arm can be moved by the rover to dig up soil or drill into rock to gather samples for the rover's other instruments to examine.

WHEELS

The rover has covered over 20 km on its six 50-cm aluminium wheels, mounted on legs that can move up and down to let the rover clamber over large rocks.

HAPPY LANDINGS

Landing rovers gently and safely is crucial to mission success. The Sojourner and Mars Exploration Rovers were cushioned by a large collection of airbags that inflated moments before the machines landed on Mars. The airbags rapidly deflated after landing, allowing the rovers to drive away over them.

The Curiosity Rover was lowered on to Mars in 2012 by the ingenious Sky Crane. This device used small rockets that fired to slow its fall down from 320 km/h to under 3 km/h. Just 12 seconds before landing, the crane winched the rover down on cables which detached once the rover detected that its wheels were touching the ground.

ASTRONAUT TRAINING

Astronaut training takes a number of years, as candidates are schooled in every aspect of their mission and the spacecraft they will travel in. They also build their survival, health and safety skills to prepare them for the demands of space. Technology often helps with all this training.

FEEL THE FORCE

During extreme changes of speed in space such as launches, astronauts can face an increase in the force of gravity (G-force) people experience on Earth. These strong forces and the effects on an astronaut's body can be simulated on Earth in a machine called a centrifuge (below).

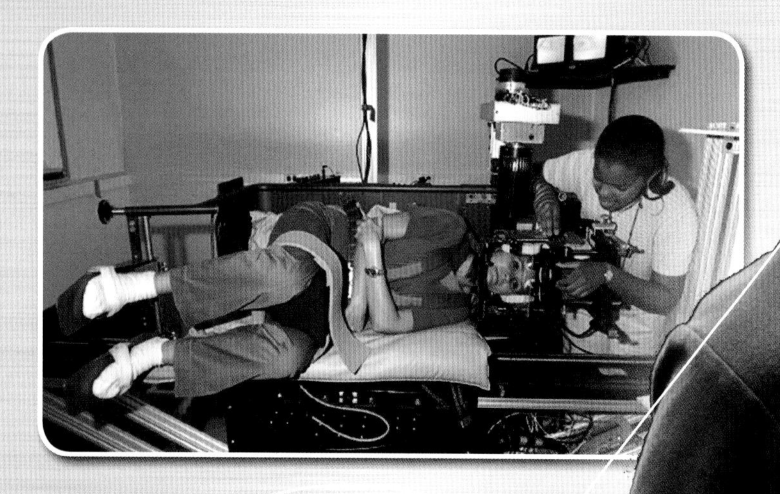

VIRTUAL TRAINING

Virtual reality (VR) is the use of computers to create a realistic virtual world which an astronaut can move round and interact with. This world is often projected on to the screens of a three-dimensional headset as worn here by NASA astronaut Suni Williams.

DEALING WITH MICROGRAVITY

Microgravity is the absence of gravity we experience on Earth. In space, this causes people and loose objects to experience weightlessness and float around. To simulate this, astronauts sometimes fly on aircraft which dive and climb sharply on parabolic flights (below). These flights produce short bursts (usually 20–30 seconds) of weightlessness.

SPACE DIVE

Another way to simulate the microgravity in space is to rehearse actions and tasks underwater. At 61.6 m long, 31.1 m wide and 12.2 m deep, NASA's Neutral Buoyancy Lab in Texas is the world's largest indoor pool. Astronauts in full EVA space suits, like Italy's Samantha Cristoforetti (above), are lowered into the pool on a ramp.

IN THE POOL

The pool contains 23.5 million litres of water, as well as realistic, full-size models of International Space Station modules and visiting spacecraft. Astronauts may spend hours in the pool, rehearsing tasks they will perform in space.

Astronauts Terry Virts and Samantha Cristoforetti simulate a trouble-shooting mission on a mock-up of the ISS in NASA's giant indoor pool.

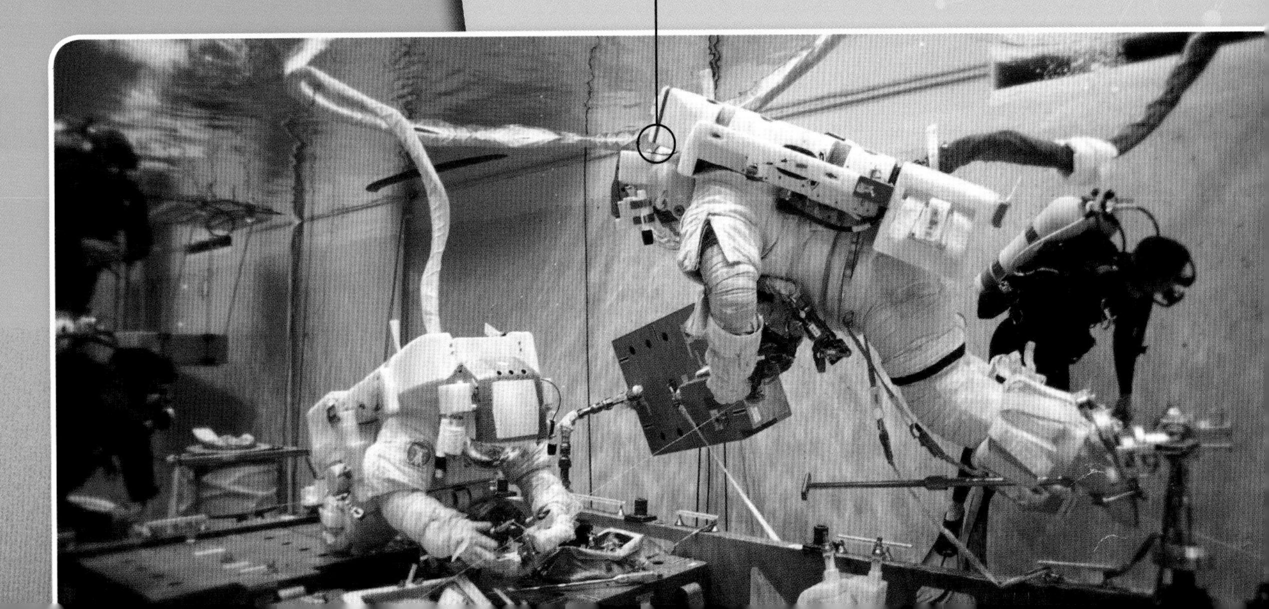

INTERNATIONAL SPACE STATION

The biggest collection of space tech in one place began as a single 4.1-m-long module, called Zarya, launched in 1998. It has grown to be 109 m long and 73 m wide – seven times bigger than Skylab. Astronauts have lived continuously on-board the International Space Station (ISS) since 2000.

RADIATORS

Unwanted heat from the ISS and all of its systems is absorbed by liquid ammonia running through tubes which travel into these large radiators. Heat leaves the tubes and heads out into space.

Astronauts working on the Mobile Remote Servicer Base System (MBS) and the Mobile Transporter on the ISS.

MODULES AND NODES

Weighing over 420 tonnes completed, the ISS was far too big and heavy to launch in one go. Instead, individual modules and linking blocks, called nodes, were launched into space and gradually assembled over more than a decade. The construction involved more than 50 space flights and 1,152 hours of spacewalks.

VISITING SPACECRAFT

Soyuz (see pages 20-21) spacecraft ferry astronauts to and from the ISS, while unmanned automated spacecraft bring food and other supplies to the station and carry away unwanted rubbish. Various spacecraft have docked with the ISS, including Cygnus, the ESA's ATV and in 2018, SpaceX's Dragon craft.

INTEGRATED TRUSS STRUCTURE

This is the 109-m-long spine of the space station to which modules and nodes were attached. It is built from aluminium and stainless steel in 10 separate sections, each flown up into space separately. The truss is covered in panels which protect interior wiring from radiation and fast-flying particles, called micrometeoroids, that whizz through space.

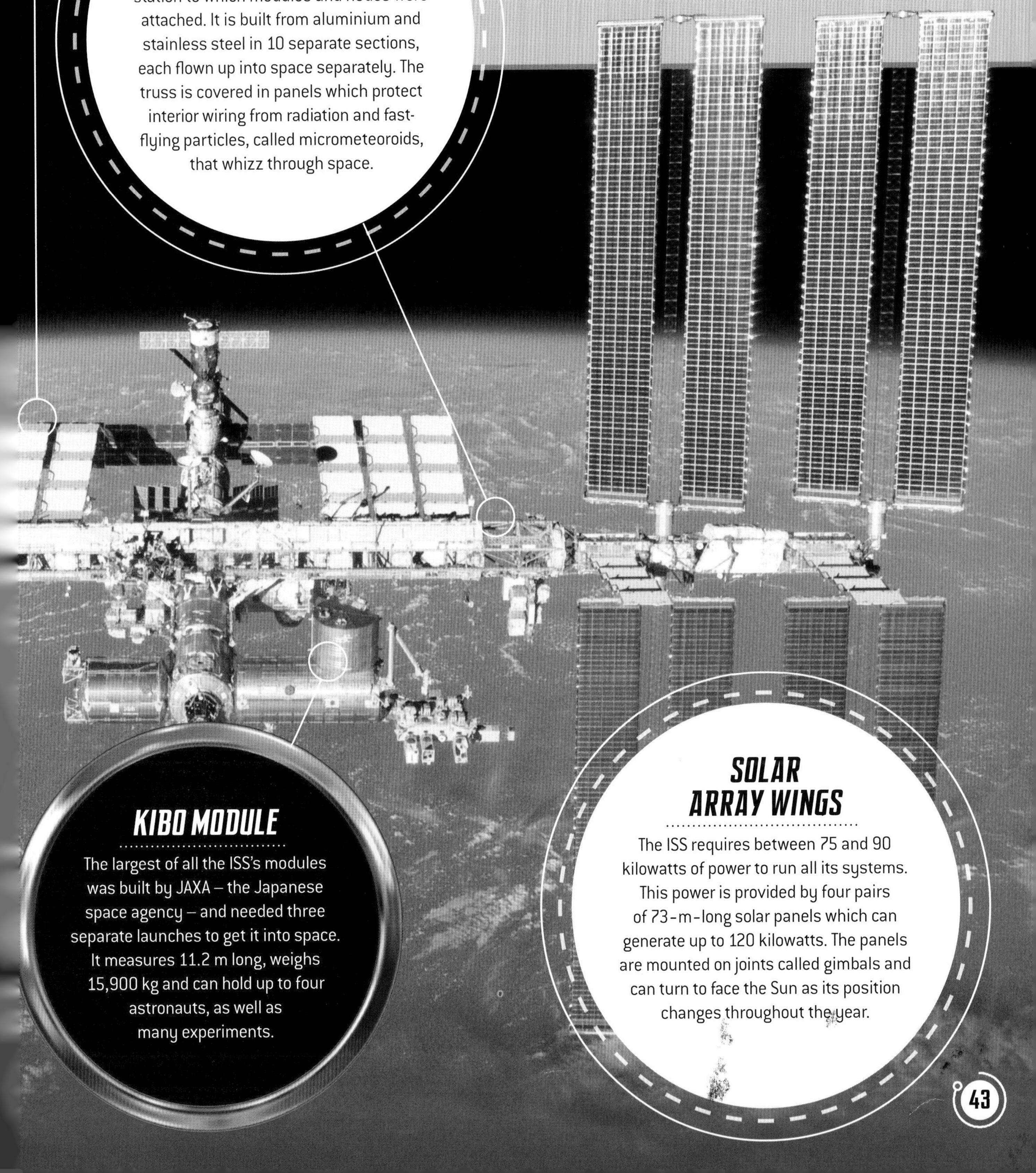

KIBO MODULE

The largest of all the ISS's modules was built by JAXA – the Japanese space agency – and needed three separate launches to get it into space. It measures 11.2 m long, weighs 15,900 kg and can hold up to four astronauts, as well as many experiments.

SOLAR ARRAY WINGS

The ISS requires between 75 and 90 kilowatts of power to run all its systems. This power is provided by four pairs of 73-m-long solar panels which can generate up to 120 kilowatts. The panels are mounted on joints called gimbals and can turn to face the Sun as its position changes throughout the year.

THE ISS AT WORK

Orbiting Earth some 400 km above the ground, the ISS needs to sustain itself for the many months between spacecraft arrivals. Air, water, food, waste and communications all need to be managed carefully, and technology plays a huge part.

ROBOT COMPANION

The latest robotic recruit to be trialled inside the ISS arrived in July 2018. Crew Interactive Mobile Companion (CIMON) is a 32-cm-wide, flying ball which responds to astronauts' voice commands. It can display or speak instructions on how to repair space station parts, as well as adjust experiments.

The Control Center in Korolev, Russia, communicates with the International Space Station crew.

COMPUTING CHECKER

More than 50 computer systems on-board the ISS help to run all of its systems and keep a constant check on every functioning part. These communicate with computers on the ground at mission control centres, whose programs are made up of more than three million lines of computer code.

ARMED UP

Several robot arms handle parts and machines on the ISS. At 17.6 m in length, Canadarm2 is the longest. The arm features seven motorised joints and can travel up and down the length of the truss on a wheeled trolley. In 2018, Canadarm2 helped the Cygnus unmanned cargo spacecraft dock with the ISS.

Astronaut Leland Melvin exercises using the Advanced Resistive Exercise Device (ARED) in the Unity node of the ISS.

BREATHE EASY

Up to 9 kg of oxygen is generated every day on the ISS by a process called electrolysis. This uses electrical power from the space station's solar panels to split water molecules into hydrogen and oxygen gas, which is added to the cabin air system.

LIFE ON BOARD

Astronauts rely on technology to live on the ISS – from heaters to warm up their pouched meals, to vacuum toilets which suck away waste, rather than flushing with water. An astronaut's muscles can waste away in microgravity, so they use technology to stay fit for two hours a day, including the ARED gym trainer, which uses air pressure to help work an astronaut's muscles.

SCIENCE IN SPACE

Dozens of experiments are run simultaneously on the ISS in different modules. The Destiny Module, for example, has storage and power facilities to hold 24 racks of scientific projects, as well as the Microgravity Science Glovebox. This is a sealed box inside which astronauts can perform experiments on bacteria, liquids or burning materials without them escaping into the rest of the space station.

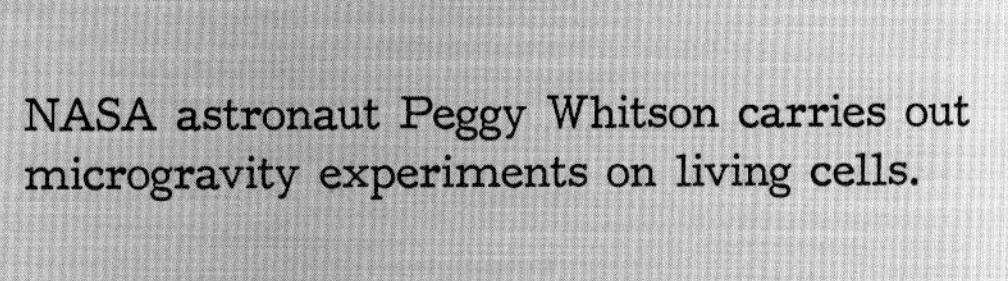

NASA astronaut Peggy Whitson carries out microgravity experiments on living cells.

PLANET HUNTER: KEPLER SPACE TELESCOPE

Named after German astronomer Johannes Kepler, the Kepler Space Telescope was sent on a mission to discover exoplanets – planets orbiting stars other than the Sun. The mission was a rousing success, discovering more than 3,924 definite exoplanets, with over 3,300 more waiting to be confirmed.

SUN SHADE

Kepler orbited the Sun, and, by mid-2018, was over 137 million km away from Earth. The Sun shade protected the photometer and other instruments inside the telescope from sunlight.

RADIATOR

The instruments inside the telescope needed to be kept really cold to work. The radiator removed heat to help keep the temperature of the parts that measured light from the stars down to -85 °C – more than four times colder than a home freezer.

LIFT-OFF

The 4.7-m-long, 2.7-m-wide telescope was launched on a Delta II rocket in 2009. Its mission was planned to last until 2013, but was extended until 2018.

PHOTOMETER

This device measured the brightness of a star. It detected a change in brightness when a planet travelled in front of the star – one of the main ways new exoplanets are detected for the first time.

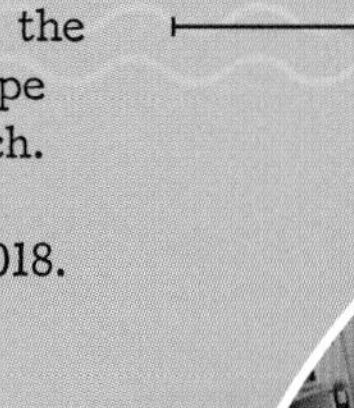

Technicians work on the Kepler space telescope before its 2009 launch. The telescope was retired in October 2018.

HIGH GAIN ANTENNA

The telescope could store information for up to 60 days before this antenna beamed the data back to Earth using radio signals.

EXOPLANETS

Discovered by the Kepler Space Telescope in 2016, the K2-33b exoplanet (below) is bigger than Neptune, but is so close to its own star that it only takes five days to complete its orbit. Scientists are searching for exoplanets that orbit Sun-like stars and possess an environment that could potentially support life.

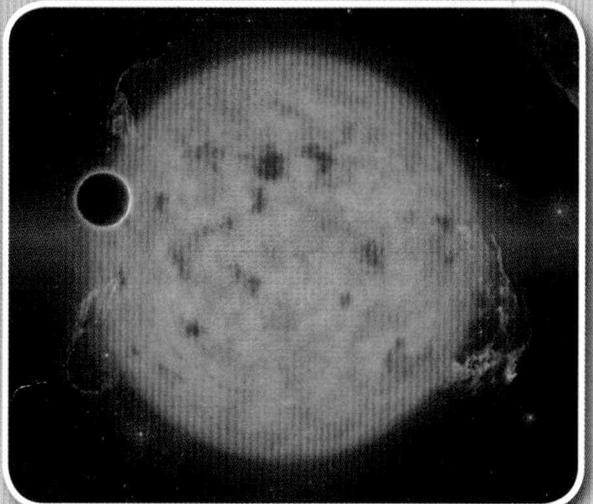

STAR TRACKERS

This pair of devices helped keep the telescope pointing in the correct direction. They monitored the positions of the stars that the telescope was to observe.

DWARF PLANET EXPLORERS

Dwarf planets are not as big as the eight planets in the Solar System, but they are not moons either, as they orbit the Sun and do not orbit a planet. There are at least five dwarf planets in the Solar System and two, Ceres and Pluto, have been recently visited by innovative space probes.

NEW HORIZONS

This lightweight (488 kg), long-distance traveller was boosted into space by a particularly powerful rocket, so that it sped away at over 58,500 km/h – the fastest a probe has ever left Earth. Even at that rapid rate New Horizons took 3,463 days to reach Pluto, going into hibernation to save power for much of the journey.

BIG DISH

Radio signals beamed back from the 2.1-m-wide dish took 4.5 hours to reach Earth. The dish was also turned into a type of radar sensor to measure details about Pluto's thin atmosphere.

RADIOACTIVE POWER PLANT

Only a thousandth of the Sun's energy the Earth receives strikes Pluto, meaning New Horizons could not rely on solar power. Instead, the piano-sized probe and its seven scientific instruments was powered by 11 kg of radioactive plutonium.

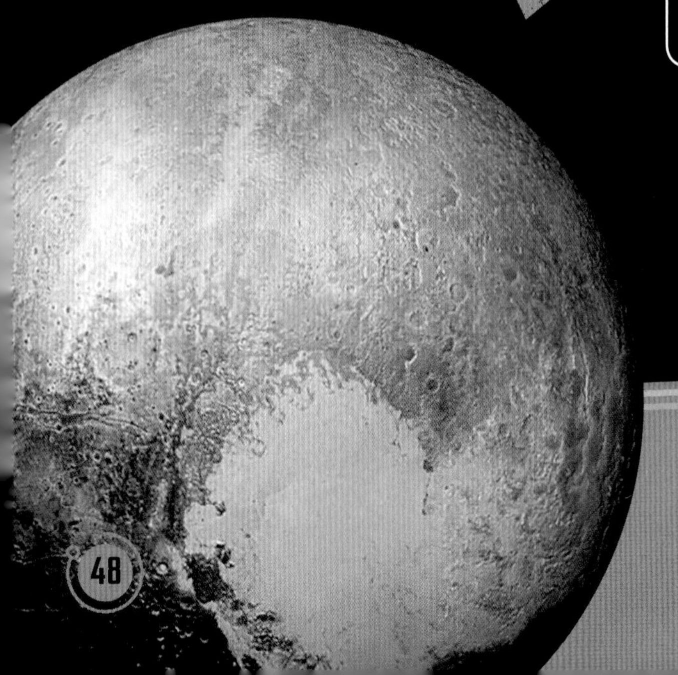

PICTURES OF PLUTO

Images of Pluto taken by telescopes had been fuzzy and indistinct before New Horizons got up close and its RALPH camera revealed a surprisingly varied and colourful surface.

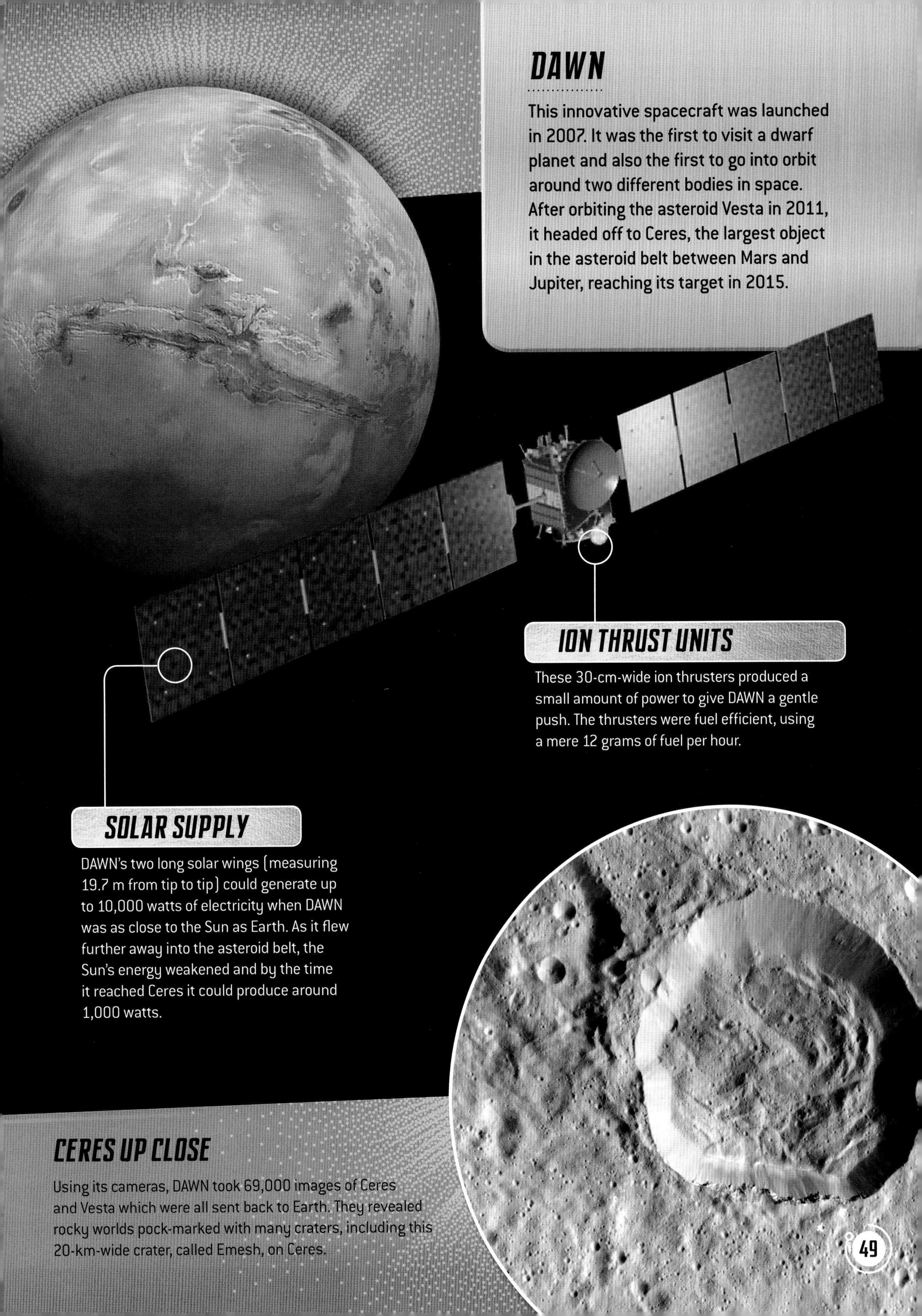

DAWN

This innovative spacecraft was launched in 2007. It was the first to visit a dwarf planet and also the first to go into orbit around two different bodies in space. After orbiting the asteroid Vesta in 2011, it headed off to Ceres, the largest object in the asteroid belt between Mars and Jupiter, reaching its target in 2015.

ION THRUST UNITS

These 30-cm-wide ion thrusters produced a small amount of power to give DAWN a gentle push. The thrusters were fuel efficient, using a mere 12 grams of fuel per hour.

SOLAR SUPPLY

DAWN's two long solar wings (measuring 19.7 m from tip to tip) could generate up to 10,000 watts of electricity when DAWN was as close to the Sun as Earth. As it flew further away into the asteroid belt, the Sun's energy weakened and by the time it reached Ceres it could produce around 1,000 watts.

CERES UP CLOSE

Using its cameras, DAWN took 69,000 images of Ceres and Vesta which were all sent back to Earth. They revealed rocky worlds pock-marked with many craters, including this 20-km-wide crater, called Emesh, on Ceres.

SUPER SCOPES

The Hubble is just one of a number of telescopes in space. Some other space telescopes don't capture light that we can see (visible light). Instead, they gather other types of energy, such as X-rays and infrared, given off by stars, galaxies and other objects in space. Just like light, these energies can be studied and turned into images.

CHANDRA X-RAY OBSERVATORY

X-rays are given off by energy-packed objects in space, such as exploding stars, called supernovas. Most X-rays are absorbed by Earth's atmosphere, so wouldn't reach telescopes on the ground. Chandra (right)was launched into space in 1999 on a distant orbit. At its furthest, it is over 130,000 km away from Earth.

BAKE OFF

Chandra's orbit is too far away for astronauts to repair or clean the telescope, so it has to look after itself. One of the telescope's imaging devices, called ASIC, has a heater that can switch on to bake away dust and other debris that collects and reduces its performance.

MOVING AROUND

Two thrusters can be commanded to fire, moving the telescope so that it points at a different part of space. The telescope is remote-controlled from Earth by mission controllers in Massachusetts, USA.

Chandra at work observing stars in a distant galaxy. The telescope orbits high above Earth, 200 times higher than the Hubble's orbit and more than one third of the way to the Moon.

This is the first map of radioactivity in a supernova remnant, the blown-out bits and pieces of a massive star that exploded. The blue colour shows radioactive material mapped in high-energy X-rays.

CRYOSTAT

This cooling device held 360 litres of liquid helium when launched. It keeps the telescope's instruments incredibly cold (as low as -272 °C) so that their own heat doesn't interfere with the infrared radiation it is observing from space.

SPITZER TELESCOPE

The Spitzer Space Telescope (above) was launched in 2003. This telescope has a diameter of 85 cm and gathers in infrared energy. This form of energy is given off as heat by bodies in space and can travel through dust and gas clouds. This means that infrared telescopes get to 'see' objects hidden to regular telescopes, such as new stars forming inside clouds of gas.

AMAZING DISCOVERIES

Spitzer has discovered new galaxies and cool and dim failed stars called brown dwarfs. It has also discovered exoplanets (see page 46–47) and another ring around the planet Saturn. In addition, the telescope has enabled astronomers to study the remains left over after a star has exploded (supernova remnants) or the gas and dust cast off by a dying star (a planetary nebula).

NASA celebrated the Spitzer Space Telescope's 12th anniversary by producing a calender containing some of the telescope's biggest discoveries and most spectacular images.

JUPITER AND SOLAR PROBES

Probes have been sent to investigate the two biggest objects in the Solar System – Jupiter and the Sun. Jupiter is the biggest planet, so large that it's twice as massive as all the other planets put together. Yet 1,000 Jupiters could fit inside the Sun, such is its size.

JUPITER PROBES

Pioneer, Ulysses and Voyager probes have all flown past Jupiter, but NASA's Galileo in 1995 was the first probe to orbit the planet. Juno was the latest Jupiter explorer and weighed 3,625 kg when launched in 2011 by an Atlas V551 rocket, fitted with five solid rocket boosters. It reached Jupiter in 2016.

An Atlas V rocket launches with the Juno spacecraft payload from Cape Canaveral Air Force Station in Florida, USA, on Friday, 5 August, 2011.

THREE WINGS

Jupiter receives only 1/25th of the energy that Earth gets from the Sun, so Juno (below) needs big solar panels to generate enough electricity for its systems. Its three 9-m-long solar panels generate a little over 400 watts.

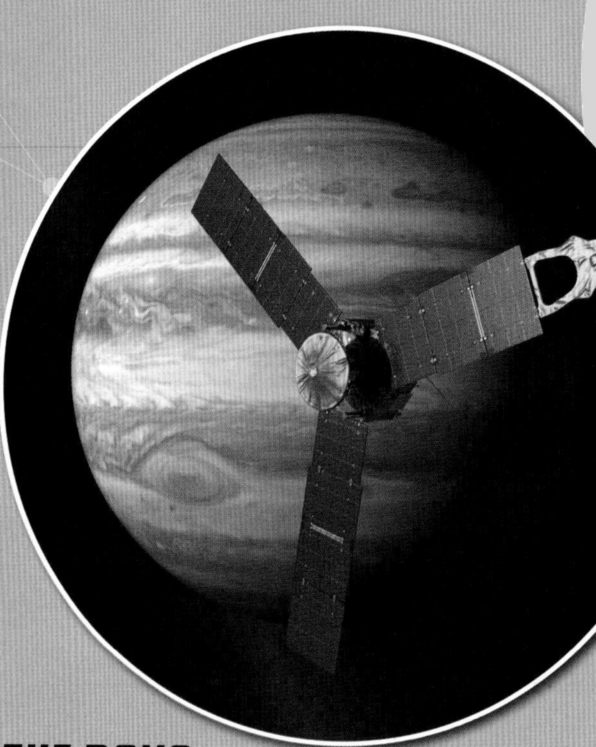

WHAT'S IN THE BOX?

Juno's 3.5-m square body is made of titanium and shields the probe's nine scientific instruments from radiation. The instruments measure Jupiter's magnetic field, the planet's gravity and the lights in its sky, called aurorae.

JUNOCAM

The JunoCam is a telescope and camera combination that has taken thousands of high-resolution photographs of Jupiter. This JunoCam image shows the swirling clouds that make up a giant storm in Jupiter's atmosphere.

The Great Red Spot, a storm the size of the Earth, rages on Jupiter.

BEAT THE HEAT

At its closest to the Sun, the Parker Solar probe will face temperatures of over 1,300 °C. It's protected from this extreme heat by a 2.4-m-diameter, 11.5-cm-thick heat shield made of carbon fibre which absorbs and reflects all the heat, so that temperatures behind the shield are just 30 °C.

PARKER SOLAR PROBE

Launched in 2018, this probe will get seven times closer to the Sun than any other probe before it to study how our closest star formed and works. To get there, the probe will fly past Venus seven times and use the planet's gravity to change its speed and the path it flies on through space.

SENDING DATA BACK

Long antennas will send back information as the probe races through space. At its closest to the Sun, the probe will be travelling at an incredibly fast 680,000 km/h – that's more than 188 km every second!

MARS 2020

The biggest and, at 1,050 kg, heaviest rover to travel to the red planet, Mars 2020 is based on the Curiosity Rover which reached Mars in 2012. This new, rugged rover is packed with science experiments and equipment to check out Mars' geology and to seek out whether substances vital to life exist on the planet.

SNAP HAPPY

Mars 2020 features 23 different cameras, many of them mounted on its 2.2-m-tall mast. Some are used to send back detailed 3D images to Earth. Others are used for navigation and to detect obstacles which the rover can avoid when on the move.

HEATED BODY

The rover's 3-m-long body features a WEB or Warm Electronics Box, which contains heaters to protect the rover's sensitive electronics from Mars' cold temperatures. These can plummet to below -120 °C.

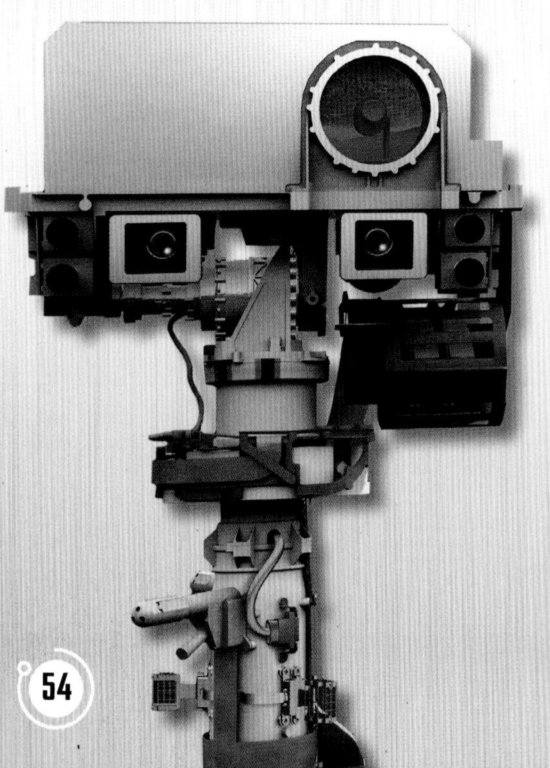

An artist's impression of the Mars Helicopter Scout being developed by NASA. The helicopter will fly on short journeys. Future space helicopters may plot routes ahead for ground rovers to travel on.

LASER VAPORISER

The SuperCam instrument fires a red laser beam that vaporises a small fragment of rock, turning it into gases. Devices called spectrometers fitted to SuperCam then analyse the gases to work out which substances the rock is made from.

MARS HELICOPTER SCOUT

A late addition to the mission, this small helicopter weighs just 1.8 kg and features a body about the size of a large orange. It will fly itself around Mars using its twin sets of rotor blades that will whizz round at speeds of 3,000 revolutions per minute.

POWERED WHEELS

Each of the rover's 52.5-cm-wide aluminium wheels is powered by its own electric motor. Fitted to legs made of titanium that are hinged and can move, these enable the rover to ride up and over rocks as tall as 78 cm.

TOOLED UP

Mars 2020 has a 2.2-m-long robot arm with a turret on its end which houses a complete tool kit. Among the cameras and chemical sensors is a small but powerful drill that can collect 60-mm-long samples of rocks.

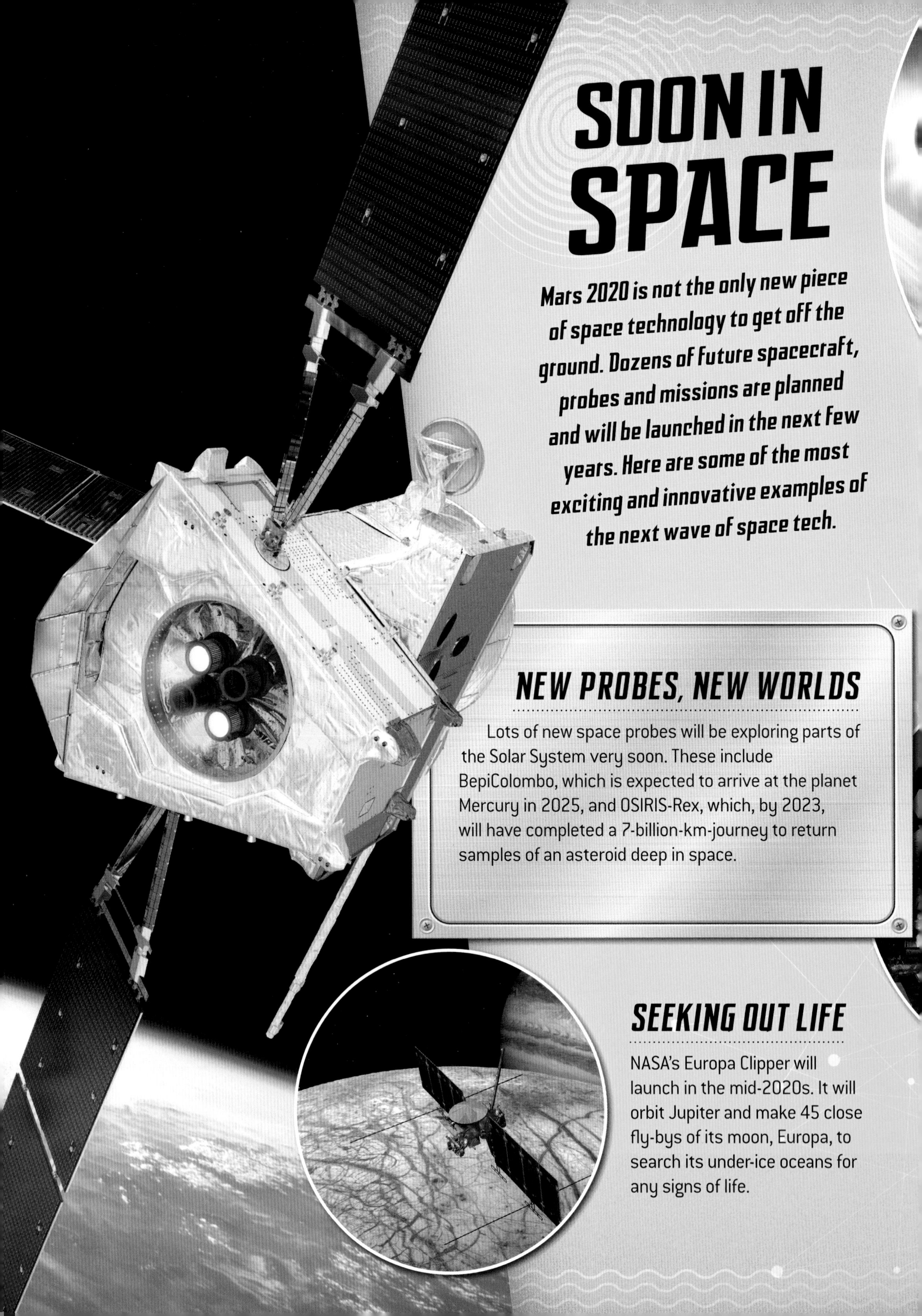

SOON IN SPACE

Mars 2020 is not the only new piece of space technology to get off the ground. Dozens of future spacecraft, probes and missions are planned and will be launched in the next few years. Here are some of the most exciting and innovative examples of the next wave of space tech.

NEW PROBES, NEW WORLDS

Lots of new space probes will be exploring parts of the Solar System very soon. These include BepiColombo, which is expected to arrive at the planet Mercury in 2025, and OSIRIS-Rex, which, by 2023, will have completed a 7-billion-km-journey to return samples of an asteroid deep in space.

SEEKING OUT LIFE

NASA's Europa Clipper will launch in the mid-2020s. It will orbit Jupiter and make 45 close fly-bys of its moon, Europa, to search its under-ice oceans for any signs of life.

ORION

NASA's Orion spacecraft (left) will be tested and launched in the 2020s. It will carry a crew of up to four astronauts on long-distance missions that may include a return to the Moon or visits to near-Earth asteroids and possibly, in the 2030s, trips to Mars.

JAMES WEBB SPACE TELESCOPE

With a light-gathering mirror over six times bigger than the Hubble, the JWST will be the largest ever space telescope when it launches in 2021. Orbiting a point 1.5 million km from Earth, its giant mirror and advanced instruments will allow astronomers to see deeper into space than ever before.

Technicians work on the segmented mirror of the JWST.

FOLD-OUT SCOPE

The JWST is so big that both its mirror (made of 18 different segments) and its heat shield, the size of a tennis court, unpack themselves and fold out to their full size once the telescope is out in space.

BACK ON EARTH

The Square Kilometre Array (SKA) is an ambitious project using thousands of radio antennas and dishes, most based in South Africa and Australia, to form a one-million-square-metre radio telescope. Such a scope could detect the faintest of radio signals and may revolutionise our knowledge of the Universe.

The central computer that controls the SKA will have the processing power of 100 million desktop PCs.

SPACE BASES

The future in space is unpredictable but exciting. New advances may make it possible to send humans to explore Mars and live in a Mars base.

GETTING TO MARS

At its closest to Earth, Mars still lies over 57 million km away. So a journey to Mars would take six months or more. A spacecraft such as Orion (see page 57) might blast off from Earth and, once in space, dock with another, larger spacecraft such as Lockheed-Martin's proposed Mars Base Camp (below) which provides living and working quarters on the long journey.

BLOW-UP BASES

Carrying large, solid, heavy structures into space is difficult. An inflatable module could pack down small and light for launch and then be blown up with air or another gas to its full size.

OXYGEN GENERATOR

An experiment on the Mars 2020 rover called MOXIE will test whether future tech on Mars can extract oxygen from the planet's atmosphere.

HABITATION MODULES

Possibly built by robots in advance of the human mission, a Mars base would need modules pressurised with air for the astronauts to breathe. It might consist of multiple modules connected by nodes, just like space stations.

MARS GREENHOUSE

Growing food on Mars would reduce the huge amounts of food supplies needed from Earth. Automated greenhouses could be set up and grow their first crops before the astronauts arrive. Already, small amounts of lettuce and cabbage have been grown under LED lights on board the ISS in an experimental greenhouse called VEGGIE.

SOLAR ARRAY

Although Mars receives less energy from the Sun than Earth, its lack of clouds means that advanced efficient solar panels might provide enough power for all the systems on a Mars base. Mobile robots might work to keep the panels clean and free of dust.

ROVING AROUND

Mars astronauts would explore the red planet in sealed and pressurised rover vehicles which might look like this concept vehicle designed by NASA in 2017. Mars rovers might dock directly with the base, allowing astronauts to travel between the two without going outside.

BUILD A ROCKET

You might not be able to launch a payload to Mars or the Moon, but this DIY rocket demonstrates the action-reaction principle that powers all space rockets. And it should, with a bit of luck, blast off fairly high into the sky.

YOU WILL NEED

1-litre plastic fizzy drinks bottle

Bottle cork, cut in half

Bicycle track pump

Pump needle adaptor (the type used to inflate a football)

Duct tape

Thick, strong, corrugated card

Sheet of thin card or sugar paper

Sticky tape

Scissors

Two same-sized blocks of wood (or other material)

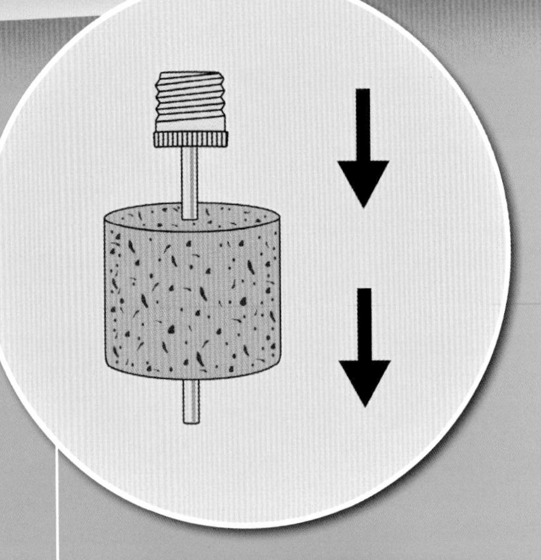

STAGE 1

Get an adult to help you drive the pump adaptor through the cork so that the air hole at the needle end pokes out fully from the surface of the cork.

STAGE 2

Fill the bottle with water and, with the bottle opening facing upwards, push the cork in really firmly. If the cork is not in tight, remove, wrap some duct tape around its sides and force it back into the bottle opening.

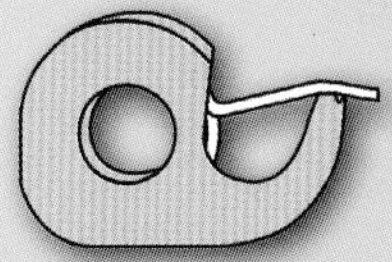

STAGE 3

Roll a cone shape out of the thin card and tape it together, so it will fit over the base of the upside-down bottle as a nose cone.

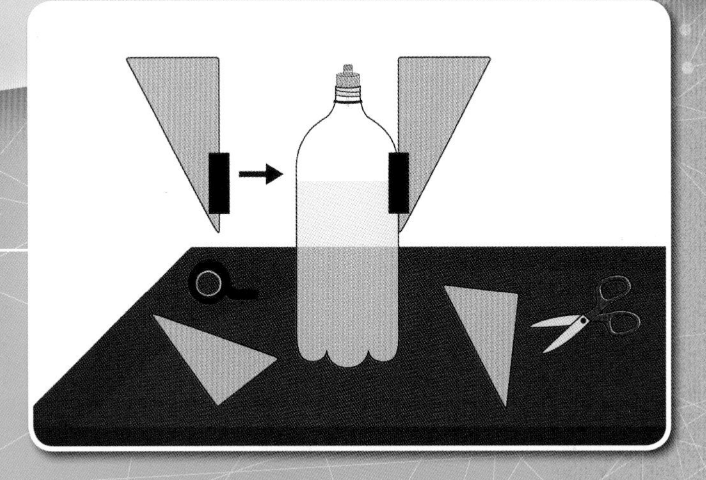

STAGE 4

Cut four identical, large, right-angled triangles out of the thick card. Use strong tape to attach these to the bottle so that they are all at the same height.

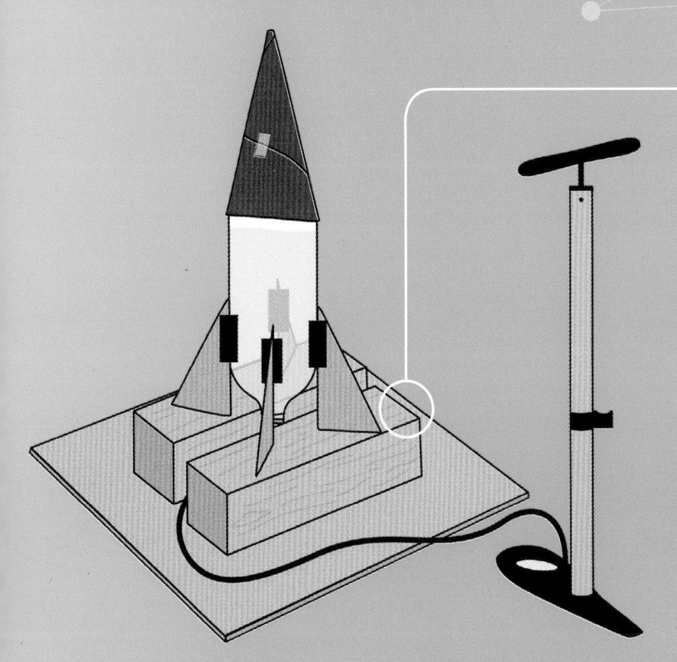

STAGE 5

Use the two blocks of wood, placed on a solid wooden board, to make your launchpad. You need to make sure there is plenty of room underneath to connect the bike pump to the adaptor. Build your launchpad in an open space where it can't do any damage to people, animals or buildings.

STAGE 6

Tightly connect the pump adaptor to the bicycle pump. Start pumping to build up the pressure in the bottle. Eventually, the pressure will force the cork out and your rocket will lift off. Expect to get wet!

GLOSSARY

alloy A combination of two or more metals or metals and another element.

ambitious An ambitious project is a difficult, advanced task or mission that needs a high level of skill to succeed.

array A number of telescopes or scientific instruments, all working together.

atmosphere The blanket of gases that surround a planet's surface.

deploy To place in position and make ready for operation.

EVA Short for extravehicular activity, a journey made outside of a spacecraft by an astronaut.

evacuate To leave quickly.

exoplanet A planet found outside of the Solar System.

galaxy A vast collection of millions of stars, planets, gas and dust, bound together by gravity.

gravity The invisible force of attraction between objects. (See also: microgravity)

infrared A type of energy that travels in waves given off by objects in space.

instrument A device that measures or records energy from astronomical objects such as stars or planets.

microgravity The very weak pull of gravity, as experienced by astronauts in space, which makes them feel weightless.

micrometeoroid A very small particle under 1 mm in size, which travels through space.

NASA Short for the National Aeronautics and Space Administration, this is the United States' major space agency.

nebula A cloud-like mass of gas and, sometimes, dust that exists in space.

nucleus In general, this means the centre of something. A comet's nucleus is a mixture of ice, dust and rock all frozen together at the centre of a comet.

orbit To travel round another object in space, usually in an elliptical path.

payload The cargo carried by a rocket or another launch vehicle from Earth into space.

radiation Energy, such as infrared, X-rays and visible light, that travels through space in waves.

revolution One 360° turn.

silica Short for silicon dioxide, this is a mineral found on Earth as part of substances such as quartz.

Soviet Union A country spanning parts of Europe and Asia from 1922 to 1991, when it broke up into Russia, Ukraine and 13 other nations.

FURTHER READING

BOOKS

It'll Never Work: Rockets and Space Travel
Jon Richards, Franklin Watts (2016)

The International Space Station
Clive Gifford, Wayland (2017)

Space Probes
Steve Parker, Franklin Watts (2015)

Machines Close-up: Space Vehicles
Daniel Gilpin and Alex Pang, Wayland (2012)

Dogs in Space: The Amazing True Story of Belka and Strelka
Victoria Southgate, Wren & Rook (2018)

Space Exploration
Giles Sparrow, Franklin Watts (2013)

WEBLINKS

https://www.esa.int/esaKIDSen/SEMVVIXJD1E_Technology_0.html
Fascinating webpages on how space launch vehicles work, produced by the European Space Agency.

http://www.nasa.gov/mission_pages/station/main/#.VDZmZfldXHk
NASA's detailed webpages on the International Space Station.

https://www.youtube.com/watch?v=7zpojhD4hpl
A fascinating lecture with great video clips by NASA engineer Kobie Boykins on how the Curiosity rover landed and works on Mars.

https://www.youtube.com/watch?v=M2_NeFbFcSw
A 20-minute video showing how a Soyuz spacecraft docks with the International Space Station, brought to you by the European Space Agency.

INDEX

Aldrin, Edward 'Buzz' 13, 16, 17
antenna 8, 11, 18, 21, 24, 25, 26, 28, 31, 36, 38, 47, 53, 57
Apollo missions 13, 14, 15, 16–17, 18–19, 22
Arecibo Observatory 33
asteroid 4, 49, 56, 57
astronaut 4, 5, 12, 13, 14, 16, 17, 18, 19, 20, 21, 22, 23, 26, 27, 29, 30, 34, 35, 40, 41, 42, 43, 44, 45, 50, 57, 58, 59
atmosphere 10, 29, 30, 35, 37, 48, 50, 53, 58
aurorae 52

Bepi-Colombo 56

camera 18, 24, 27, 33, 38, 48, 49, 53, 54, 55
Canadarm2 45
Cape Canaveral Air Force Station 7, 52
capsule 10, 11
Cassini-Huygens 36, 37
centrifuge 40
Ceres 48, 49
Chandra X-ray Observatory 50
combustion 6
comet 4, 36, 37
computer 12, 17, 20, 21, 24, 29, 32, 35, 40, 44, 57
Conrad, Charles, Jr. 23
Cooper, Gordon 12
Cristoforetti, Samantha 41
Cygnus 43, 45

DAWN 49
dock 17, 21, 22, 43, 45, 58, 59
dwarf planet 48, 49

ejection seat 10
electricity 20, 23, 30, 49, 52
EMU (Extravehicular Mobility Unit) 26
engine 4, 6, 7, 8, 10, 11, 12, 14, 15, 16, 17, 19, 29, 34, 37
F1 rocket engine 14, 15
ESA (European Space Agency) 4, 43
Europa Clipper 56
EVA (extravehicular activity) 5, 13, 41
exoplanet 46, 47, 51
experiment (scientific) 22, 23, 43, 44, 45, 54, 58, 59
Explorer 1 9

food (in space) 9, 23, 43, 44, 59
fuel 6, 7, 8, 10, 14, 15, 17, 21, 49

Gagarin, Yuri 10, 11, 12
Galileo 52
Gemini missions 12–13
Goddard, Robert 7
golden disk 25
gravity 40, 41, 52, 53
Great Dark Spot 24
Great Red Spot 53

helmet 27
Hubble Space Telescope 30–31, 35, 50, 57

Jade Rabbit 2 5
James Webb Space Telescope 57
JunoCam 53
Jupiter 25, 49, 52, 53, 56

Kepler Space Telescope 46–47
kerosene 14

Laika 9
laser 39, 55
launch 4, 5, 6, 7, 8, 9, 10, 12, 14, 15, 20, 21, 22, 23, 24, 28, 30, 34, 40, 42, 43, 46, 47, 49, 50, 51, 52, 53, 56, 57, 58
Lunar Rover 18–19
Lunokhod 18

Mars 4, 38, 39, 49, 54, 55, 56, 57, 58, 59
Mars 2020 54–55, 56, 58
Mars Base Camp 58
Mars Helicopter Scout 55
Mars Rover 38, 39, 54–55, 58, 59
Melvin, Leland 45
Mercury missions 12–13
microgravity 22, 23, 41, 45
Mir 23
mission control 11, 18, 44, 50
module 5, 10, 11, 13, 16, 17, 18, 20, 21, 22, 23, 35, 41, 42, 43, 45, 58
Moon (Earth's moon) 5, 13, 14, 16, 17, 18, 19, 50, 57
moon 18, 25, 36, 37, 38, 48, 56
Moon rock 19
MOXIE 58

NASA (National Aeronautics and Space Administration) 4, 7, 12, 13, 15, 18, 24, 26, 29, 34, 40, 41, 45, 51, 52, 55, 56, 57, 59
nebula 31, 51
Neptune 24, 25, 47
New Horizons 48
Newton, Isaac (Sir) 6
nitrogen 9, 10

observatory 22, 32, 33, 50
orbit 4, 7, 8, 9, 10, 15, 16, 20, 21, 22, 28, 29, 30, 34, 36, 37, 44, 46, 47, 48, 49, 50, 52, 56, 57
Orion 7, 57, 58
OSIRIS-Rex 56
oxygen 6, 9, 10, 13, 14, 15, 16, 26, 27, 45, 58

parabolic flight 41
parachute 10, 12, 16, 36
Parker Solar Probe 53
payload 6, 7, 10, 15, 35, 52
periscope 12
photovoltaic cells 23
Pioneer 52
Pluto 48
pressure 11, 12, 45
probe 4, 24, 25, 34, 36, 37, 38, 48, 52, 53, 56

radiation 26, 43, 51, 52
radioactivity 51
radio telescope 32–33, 57
radio transmitter 8, 9
radio waves 24, 32
robot 5, 26, 38, 39, 44, 45, 55, 58, 59
rocket 4, 6–7, 8, 10, 12, 14–15, 22, 34, 39, 46, 48, 52
Ariane 5 4
Atlas V 52
Delta II 46
Delta IV Heavy 7
R-7 8
Saturn V 14–15, 22
Vostok 8K72K 10
Rosetta-Philae 37
Russia 8, 23, 45

SAFER system 27
satellite 4, 7, 8, 9, 28–29, 34
Saturn 25, 36, 37, 51
Second World War 7
Shepard, Alan 12
shield 9, 10, 52, 53, 57
Sky Crane 39
Skylab 15, 22–23, 42
solar panel 4, 18, 20, 30, 38, 43, 45, 52, 59
Soviet Union 8, 11, 23
Soyuz spacecraft 20–21, 43
space shuttle 15, 29, 34–35
space station 15, 20, 21, 22–23, 34, 35, 41, 42–43, 44–45, 58
space suit 5, 11, 12, 26–27, 41
spacewalk see 'EVA'
Spitzer Space Telescope 51
Sputnik 8–9
Square Kilometre Array 57
star 4, 31, 32, 33, 46, 47, 50, 51, 53
Sun 18, 22, 24, 25, 26, 27, 30, 43, 46, 47, 48, 49, 52, 53, 59
supernova 31, 50, 51

telescope 4, 22, 30–31, 32–33, 34, 35, 46–47, 48, 50–51, 53, 57
Tereshkova, Valentina 11
thrust 6, 7, 15, 49

Ulysses 52
Universe 4, 24, 31, 57
Uranus 25
USA 7, 8, 28, 33, 50, 52

V2 rocket-powered missile 7
Velcro 19
Very Large Array 33
Virts, Terry 41
Vostok 10–11
Voyager (1 and 2) 24–25, 52

White, Ed 13
Whitson, Peggy 45
Williams, Suni 40

Yutu see 'Jade Rabbit 2'